The Living Swamp

A. Borgioli and G. Cappelli

ORBIS PUBLISHING · London

English translation © Orbis Publishing Limited, London 1979
© Istituto Geografico De Agostini S.p.A., Novara 1978
Printed in Italy by IGDA, Officine Grafiche, Novara
ISBN 0 85613 012 5

Endpapers: a flamingo colony in the Ngorongoro reserve, Tanzania
Frontispiece: a view of the valley of fish (Valle Santa) a few minutes after sunrise

Contents

Chapter One
The Environment
Page 7

Chapter Two
The Marsh Microcosm
Page 37

Chapter Three
The Lords of the Marsh
Page 65

Chapter Four
The World's Wetlands
Page 93

Geographical Index
Species Index
Page 118

Chapter One
The Environment

*Marshlands are invaluable to naturalists as places
where life and reproduction are at their most intense, forming a vital record
of the history of evolution. This introductory chapter discusses the various
kinds of wetlands which occur throughout the world
and goes on to describe the wide range of plant life
which is to be found in them.*

Imagine a small, marshy area near forest land; little more than a pool of water, unnamed and unmarked on any map. If we take a few steps among the reeds and marshy grasses we sink into the water, almost covered with water-plants, through which we may catch a glimpse of the pool bed, darkened by decomposing organic remains.

The water is quite still in the twilight of the dawn and swarms with tiny brown, comma-shaped creatures only a few millimetres in length. From time to time one of these creatures surfaces and floats motionless on the water. Suddenly one which has remained immobile for longer than the others begins to undergo an unexpected transformation. The skin on the upper part of the back in the region of the thorax starts to split, imperceptibly at first, but increasingly more markedly. A greyish, ill-defined creature emerges. First of all the curved back, then the head with its pair of greenish eyes and finally the rest of the body rises from the surface of the water vertically, like a submarine periscope. The shape gradually becomes clearer. A long proboscis, which until now has remained folded alongside the body, becomes extended. Two hairy antennae straighten up and the legs and wings quickly spread, while the liquid with which the chrysalis was impregnated dries.

And so a mosquito is born. Just one of the innumerable swarms of similar or identical mosquitoes. For a moment it remains delicately balanced on the surface of the water, then flies off to find a safer resting place. Our meeting with the marsh world starts with an apparently commonplace event being continually repeated at all latitudes and in various climates, from the plains of the far north to both temperate and tropical marshes. This is a highly significant event, for it conditions Man's present and future attitudes to marsh environment.

All of us are aware of the diseases carried by mosquitoes; but the establishment of the existence of a link between certain species of mosquito and the spread of certain diseases is relatively recent. The whole question was shrouded in mystery during antiquity; no one progressed further than the formulation of hypotheses, which were credible to a greater or lesser extent, and the story of Man's relationship with these unpleasant creatures is lost in the mists of time. Centuries before the Christian epoch in Europe, and in particular along the Mediterranean coasts, a scourge was unleashed that had already claimed countless victims in Africa and Asia. People were struck by a sudden, high fever which was inevitably fatal. The most affected were the populations living just above sea level, particularly those not far from marshes, fens or areas of stagnant water.

In his dissertation on epidemics, Hippocrates describes this scourge which developed so violently in good weather conditions. He distinguishes between fevers quickly leading to death and those coming in periodic bouts which were not always fatal, although their victims were left quite exhausted. Marcus Aurelius and the early physicians Aulus Celsus and Galen write of these fevers, which had become widespread and evolved into important social phenomena. So much so that the Romans even built temples in which prayers for salvation could be offered when the disease was at its height. The poet Horace testifies that on such occasions those who could afford to first went to pray and then left town to take refuge in higher places where the disease could not reach them. They returned to the plains and towns only when the danger had passed.

The writer who formulated a hypothesis nearer to the truth is without a doubt the Roman scholar Marcus Varro: 'Do not build farms in the vicinity of marshlands', he admonished, 'because when they dry up they generate a multitude of minute insects.' These creatures, invisible to the human eye, were picked up in the air and thus introduced into the nostrils and mouths of humans, thereby causing high fevers. Other writers did not accept the hypothesis of microscopic insects and maintained instead that the cause of the illness lay in the unwholesome mists pervading the marshes.

Time passed and Varro's theory was forgotten, but the theory that the disease was caused by bad air, 'mal aria', rising from the marshes was to persist for many centuries and it is this name – malaria – which has remained with us. For a long time science was unable to make any progress in learning either the cause or the cure for the illness. Only towards the middle of the seventeenth century was quinine – an extract of the bark of the quinquina tree – imported into Europe from Peru, where it was already in use by the Incas to cure fever attacks. Regrettably, although it cured the symptoms it did not remove the cause of the illness, which still remained a mystery. To arrive at the dis-

Facing page sequence showing the final transformation of a mosquito from the pupa stage to the imago

8

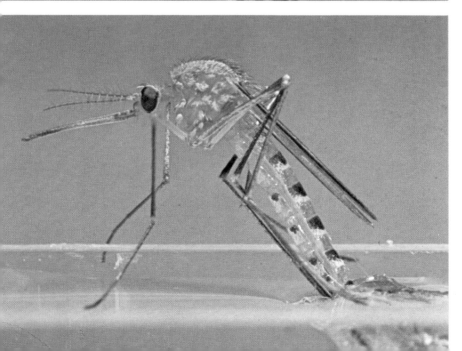

covery of the cause, it was necessary to wait until the end of the nineteenth century when research by doctors and scientists proved conclusively that micro-organisms (protozoa) of the genus *Plasmodium* were the cause of malaria; this is transmitted to human blood through the bite of a variety of mosquito species. At that time, the commonest European species, also prevalent in various regions of Asia and North Africa, was the spotted-wing mosquito (*Anopheles maculipennis*) – now practically extinct; in addition to this there are about seventy species of *Anopheles* throughout the world able to transmit the malarial plasmodia.

The idea that malaria was in some way connected with marshy environments was popular from ancient times, even if the blame was mistakenly placed on the unhealthy air. Given this situation, there were only two possible reactions: either to flee from the marshes as far as possible or to eliminate them by draining. In this way the idea of reclamation began quite early in the history of civilization.

Drainage work has continued throughout the world this century, though no longer with the sole purpose of combating malaria but motivated by a number of other forces, including a desire for land in times of grain shortage. The same course was pursued, at least in part, even after the Second World War, despite increasing evidence that much of the land reclamation was producing very little economic return and in some cases the direct or indirect damage to the ecology of the environment greatly outweighed any immediate advantage.

It is paradoxical that the mosquito caused the peoples of ancient civilizations to drain the land in order to eliminate malaria and thus indirectly caused them to destroy much marshland, but on the other hand it also prevented Man from penetrating other similar areas, which have consequently been preserved intact for the naturalist.

We can see from ancient manuscripts that Man has been plagued by mosquitoes since the earliest times. According to Herodotus, the Egyptians had various ways of warding off attacks; people living upstream of the marsh slept in towers which they had built because the wind prevented the mosquitoes from flying above ground level, while those living actually in the marsh adopted a different method in that they each had a net which they used during the day for fishing and at night as protection against the mosquitoes. It would, nevertheless, be wrong to say that apart from the nuisance factor and the problem of malaria, mosquitoes presented a serious obstacle to human settlement, at least in Europe and the temperate regions of the world.

The situation in other parts was, however, very different. Some accounts of journeys in regions of the far north are almost beyond belief. The nineteenth-century British naturalists William Kirby and William Spence, for example, describe a swarm of mosquitoes in Lapland so dense that it resembled a snowstorm or a dust-cloud whipped up by the wind. They also say that the Lapps could not eat a single mouthful of food or settle down to sleep without first fumigating their huts in order to suffocate the mosquitoes. Outside it was impossible to breathe without mosquitoes filling the nose and mouth. At least one member of a nineteenth-century expedition to the North Pole was forced to abandon his work in the Davis Straight, 72° north, because of the number of mosquitoes that plagued him incessantly. It is impossible to describe the size and vicious-ness of the swarms which attack the people of Alaska, and the inhabitants of Labrador or New Jersey will insist there is nothing to compare with the mosquitoes found in these regions.

But, by all accounts, the record goes to certain areas of the Everglades in Florida. The number of mosquitoes in Madeira Bay and surrounding areas in the month of June may well depend solely on the amount of space available. These mosquitoes do more than merely sting their victims: they directly impair their breathing. There are instances of people who have died following a mosquito attack in which life was literally sucked from them. According to James S. Haeger of the Entomological Research Centre, at Florida's Vero Beach, there are more factors involved in a mosquito attack than might be expected. He believes these fatalities are due to a number of secondary effects: the loss of liquid from the body, an allergy to the saliva injected by the insects, respiratory damage caused by physical obstruction of the passages and irritation of the mucous membrane. It is therefore not surprising that all this, combined with the panic which

Below a mirror image indicates how still and clear swamp water can be

victims of an attack experience, may result in tragedy. There is an account of a motorist who stopped to mend a puncture, was engulfed by a cloud of mosquitoes and tried to run to the nearest town for help. He was found the next morning dead by the roadside.

Despite such cases, there is some argument for the mosquito being responsible for the preservation of some of the finest and most typical parts of the Everglades, which would otherwise have been destroyed or altered completely by 'civilization' and human ignorance and greed. It is certainly true that of all the various types of natural environment which have been settled by Man and which are constantly being reshaped by him, those in greatest danger are the marshlands. And yet these areas are invaluable to naturalists as places where life and reproduction are at their most intense and as a vital record of the history of evolution.

Scientists and naturalists were, understandably enough, first to advocate the immediate conservation of marshes and similar areas, but this idea has fortunately now become a matter for public debate and even, in a few rare cases, for political action to stop further damage.

It is little wonder, therefore, that one ecologist has described the drainage of a marsh in order to exterminate the mosquitoes as being like destroying a bookcase in order to kill the mites living in it. Another naturalist, Leon Lippens, compared the drainage of Spain's Guadalquivir marshes in order to grow rice with the destruction of Chartres Cathedral and all its treasures in order to plant potatoes on the site.

Few people are aware that in 1971 an international conference was held on these initiatives at Ramsar in Iran. The result was a convention on the major areas of wetland of international importance, which is intended to provide for the conservation of those regions particularly important as the natural habitat of water and marsh birds. The convention defines the sorts of environment which are to be protected as follows: 'The wetlands in question are marshy, fen or boggy areas or any expanse of water, whether natural or artificial, permanent or seasonal, still or running, fresh, brackish or salt, including stretches of sea water not greater than six metres in depth at low tide.'

Below in the Camargue Regional Park at the mouth of the Rhône river, France

Although marshes in the true sense and similar areas (fens, bogs, swamps, etc.) are the main elements, these wet regions also include non-marshy areas (lakes, rivers, coastal inlets less than 6 m in depth etc.) which are, however, inhabited by the same fauna as the marshes themselves. Thus some species of gull may be found, again depending on the season, along the entire course of a river or on inland lakes, as well as on the coast or on actual marshes. In Europe, coot are also as common on inland lakes as on coastal marshes and the same applies to numerous other bird species.

The protection envisaged under the Ramsar convention would, therefore, extend to the following wetland environments: stagnant marshy pools filled only with water at certain times; stagnant pools which permanently contain water; marshes, large areas of permanent and seasonal stagnant pools, with emergent and also arboreal vegetation; bogs, areas where humus has accumulated, generally located in dips in the ground where water has settled; lagoons, stretches of salt or brackish water enclosed by land but either connected to or just separated from the sea; fishing beds, stretches of water in coastal regions with varying degrees of salinity and used mainly for fish farming; mangrove swamps, areas of tropical vegetation which either emerges from the water or is submerged by the tide; large inland lakes (with a surface area greater than 3 sq km); small inland lakes (with a surface area less than 3 sq km); coastal lakes situated not more than 10 km from the sea coast, whether directly connected to it or not; mountain lakes situated at least 750 m above sea level; river banks and beds; river deltas and river estuaries.

Other areas in this category might include canals, salt-pans, flood sluices or overflow basins (i.e. man-made basins for controlling the river flow), which, though artificial, make an ideal habitat for numerous marshland species, both animal and vegetable.

Even without visiting an actual marsh, fen or bog, it is possible to observe the infinite variety of creatures, in particular the migratory birds, which live in these artificial wetlands. In any case a classification of the above type does not reflect the true picture. Nature does not leap

A pool among the pine trees in the Coto Doñana reserve at the mouth of the Guadalquivir river in Spain

from one clearly defined category to another, nor can any environment exist in total isolation. This means, for example, that there might be a swamp in the true sense along the edge of a lake, but it may be there at all only because the lake itself is fed by a number of tributaries.

On the other hand, the fact that environments with certain common features lie adjacent to one another may well result in some interchange of animal and plant life, and it will be possible to observe some species on the very edges of these zones.

Although all these types of environment are of interest and consequently worth preserving, swamps and other marshy areas are by far the most fascinating, due to their wild, almost primeval nature. There are few other habitats where so manifest a feeling of close contact with nature can be experienced in such apparent isolation. All around there is noise, interspersed with periods of silence; it is close at hand but somehow it is impossible to locate its source or even the direction from which it comes.

There is something timeless about a marsh seen from a distance, the reeds waving rhythmically in the wind. An observation of a marsh through the seasons would soon dispel any preconceptions that it looks the same year in year out and is unlikely ever to change.

In actual fact there are few other types of environment which undergo such relatively rapid changes as the swamplands. They are born, they evolve and they die. The gradual accumulation of alluvial deposits can slow the flow of a river and cause a marsh to form. Subsequent deposits can then bury the marsh and it disappears.

How do marshes come into being? A geologist would say that marshes form in depressions in land not sufficiently deep to become lakes, or on the low-lying banks of lakes, rivers or seas, where marsh vegetation begins to grow; or, in very humid climates where there is a high, steady rainfall, areas which do not drain quickly may become marshes.

A considerable amount of swampland is found in coastal regions where the land is protected in some way from the breaking waves. For example, the motion of the current may build up a sandbank, behind which a lagoon may then form. On the other hand, it may be that slow subsidence of a section of coast can cause the ground to become progressively wetter, or the same may happen if the level of

the sea bed near the coast were to rise. If the coastal area is flat and there are no, or only very few, high tides, it is only a question of time before a marsh forms. Conversely, high tides and strong waves prevent plants growing.

There is one particular type of marine swamp where reeds and marsh grasses grow (*Juncus, Spartina,* etc.) which is often associated with a lagoon. The formation of this lagoon itself may depend on the conjunction of several different factors. In the Adriatic, for example, lagoons probably formed as a result of the slow but gradual sinking of the coast over many thousands of years. Others may result from the accumulation of debris brought down by a river, subsequently causing a lagoon to form at the mouth. These types of lagoon have only a limited life. This explains how a marsh may disappear, either buried under excess sediment, or eroded away as protective barriers are demolished by the sea. In Italy, the large lagoons formerly found around Pisa and Ravenna were gradually filled in and buried by deposits from rivers in flood, while some sections of the western coast of Europe provide dramatic examples of the havoc this flooding and erosion can cause. Holland, in particular, was forced to build huge artificial dykes for protection.

The Venice lagoon, on the other hand, is almost unique in that it has remained practically unchanged since 1300. It should not, however, be forgotten that this is due to careful control of the water. The rivers which flowed into the lagoon were diverted elsewhere, thus eliminating the danger of the lagoon being buried and also removing the malaria hazard, as the mosquito does not breed in salt-water. The sandbars and breakwaters were reinforced and the grass banks of the lagoon maintained intact at all times, so that the water would break evenly over them at high tide. The canals leading to the lagoon were dredged regularly, which also aided water traffic. Severe punishment was meted out by the city fathers to anyone who dared change or even interfere with this system of water control.

Unfortunately the Venetians did not maintain the system, but instead actively destroyed it. They drained a considerable number of the lagoon banks in order to reclaim land for the industrial towns of Mestre and Porto Marghera. The effects were soon felt. The tides could no longer flow freely over the banks and this meant that high waters were much more frequent.

Above dense marsh vegetation on an Alaskan lake

Facing page water buttercups in a spring scene on the Guadalquivir marshes in Spain

The calm, shallow waters of a lagoon suit a particular type of vegetation which grows on the banks and the area gradually becomes a marsh. The same marsh may, however, form even if there is no lagoon, especially if the coast is flat and the waters are shallow for some distance out to sea. In the St. Lawrence Gulf in Canada there are several miles of marsh running along the sea coast between Havre-Saint-Pierre and Mingan, while on the eastern coast of the Baltic there are sea marshes in almost every gulf or bay. The St. Lawrence Gulf has tides of almost two metres but there are practically no tides at all in the Baltic.

There are certain plant varieties which grow in such areas, gradually covering the ground with algae and sea plants, such as *Zostera*, found on the submerged parts, and reeds, grasses and rushes (*Juncus, Phragmites, Spartina*) growing on those parts not under water. This vegetation provides a base on which debris can accumulate, producing a layer of soil rich in organic material and up to several metres in depth. If the land is slowly subsiding the depth may increase to compensate for this gradual fall in the level of the ground. Conversely, the water may win in the end and the marsh disappears buried under debris from the sea.

The sea marshes which form near actual lagoons are at the centre of a delicately balanced system which itself is a unique environment with a great many interesting facets. Every lagoon consists of banks enclosing pools of water, channels, underwater sandbanks and submerged sections which become visible only at low tide. The banks comprise a line of islands often connected to the shore by a narrow strip of land, making a virtual peninsula. The bank generally runs parallel to the coast and, though never more than a few hundred metres wide, it can be several kilometres long. Basically it is a sand-dune; an accumulation of debris from the sea, bonded together by grasses (*Ammophila*). Once the dune has become established trees begin to grow, especially junipers (*Juniperus macrocarpa* and *J. communis*) and later pines (*Pinus halepensis, P. pinea*) which may eventually be sufficiently numerous to form a wood. Without this vegetation the bank would disintegrate and there would no longer be any lagoon. The banks acts as a sort of natural dyke which appears somewhat insecure but is, in fact, considerably more robust than many man-made dykes.

The lagoon itself lies in the shelter of this bank. Water from the sea flows in through channels or inlets in the bank. In some cases the level may rise and fall with the tide. Water comes in through the inlets, slowly filling up the basin, and as the tide ebbs the water flows out again. This means that water is continually flowing through what eventually becomes a maze of natural channels and the constant movement keeps the channels free.

Where there is less movement of the water in and out of the lagoon, as is generally the case in the Mediterranean, the inlets gradually become blocked with sand and the lagoon is eventually cut off completely from the sea. The salt is slowly lost from the sea-water and the lagoon becomes a freshwater pond. It is only in regions where evaporation is rapid, such as the African coast, that the reverse happens: the water slowly turns more and more salty and the lagoon becomes a natural salt-pan.

The continuous flow of the tides is vital to the animal and plant life of the lagoon. It helps the nutrients circulate and washes out debris. Most of the algae which grow in the lagoon are quickly accepted by the other organisms living there, such as the bacteria, fungi and numerous creatures – molluscs, crustacea and vertebrates, including many different species of fish and birds.

The continuous ebbing and flowing of the tides impedes the growth of vegetation and there are few algae visible to the naked eye. Plankton, which represent the first link in the food-chain, are, however, extremely prolific.

The bottom of the lagoon can be anything from a few inches to about five or six feet below sea level and, although the channels are slightly deeper, they too are still fairly shallow. It is covered with a more or less even layer of soft mud, which is often rich in organic material but is black and has an unpleasant smell. Although the channels remain permanently under water there are other submerged parts of the lagoon which are exposed during the low equinoctial tides, though of course this happens only a few times a year. But it changes the whole appearance of the lagoon. The parts which emerge from the water, known as 'velme', are like shoals or islands of mud separated by channels; their surface is flat and generally covered with a layer of vegetation or microscopic algae, zostera or other plants which grow in sea mud. The accumulation of decomposing organic matter encourages a proliferation of animal and bacteria life and it makes an ideal habitat for Mollusca and Crustacea.

In addition to these mud islands, there are other flat shoals just slightly above sea level which are exposed at low tide but covered by the water at high tide. The vegetation growing there consists mainly of marsh samphires (*Salcornia herbacea* and *S. fruticosa*), sea aster and sea meadow grasses.

Below the common reed is found growing in some profusion on waterlogged land

The samphires and other halophytes – plants which tolerate salty soil – are particularly interesting. It was once thought that they preferred only a saline environment, even though salt is generally very harmful to plants. An experiment, however, proved that the plants in question grow equally well in a soil containing no salt. It was therefore concluded that this species was particularly hardy and had managed to adapt to the presence of salt in the soil. In actual fact the plants live under unique conditions: they are flooded twice daily by salt-water and, even though surrounded by so much water, they would probably not absorb sufficient liquid for their requirements if they had not been able to make this adaptation successfully. The majority of plants are unable to absorb salt-water because of its high osmotic pressure. The water entering the lagoon has an osmotic pressure of approximately 23 atmospheres, whereas that of the tissue of most land plants is around 10 to 20 atmospheres. As it is the osmotic ratio which controls the absorption of liquid by the roots, such plants could not absorb enough liquid from salt-water and would therefore die of thirst.

Because of the accumulation of mineral salts

Left the yellow flower of the flag iris which blooms in spring

Below marsh samphires are common in the brackish waters of the Venice lagoons

and similar substances (sugars) in their tissues, halophytes, on the other hand, are able to increase their own osmotic pressure considerably beyond the level of that of sea-water and can therefore absorb it with ease. They can reach an osmotic pressure of about 100 atmospheres; and that of the American varieties can even rise to 180 atmospheres, which means they can survive in environments where evaporation causes a considerable increase in salt content.

Even though they grow in very wet or marshy areas, the halophytes are similar in appearance to plants which live in arid regions, in particular the grasses. Unfortunately the mechanism by which they absorb the salt-water may sometimes backfire and cause the death of an entire species. What happens is that the osmotic pressure of the root tissues becomes so high that, should they then find themselves in much weaker salt solution than that to which they are accustomed, they absorb more water than they require and die.

A variety of plant species grows at the edges of the lagoon or in the less salty parts, for example *Juncus maritimus*, and reeds such as *Phragmites*. The vegetation is therefore the same as that found in freshwater marshes. Plants which live semi-submersed in water, such as *Spartina*, can spread over a wide area and is for the most part fairly monotonous. But at the end of the summer the leaves change colour, giving the marsh a reddish tinge.

Another type of sea marsh is the mangrove swamp, distinct from other coastal marshes in that the dense and rapid-growing vegetation acts as a binder for the muddy ground and spreads out, reclaiming land from the sea. They are found in tropical and sub-tropical regions – in Africa in the Gulf of Guinea, Nigeria, Gabon, the Cameroons, Zaire, Kenya and Mozambique; in Asia along the coasts of Indonesia and Malaysia and in the Sonda archipelago; on the northern coast of Australia, New Guinea and Molucca; in America in the Everglades in Florida, along the Atlantic coast of Central America; in Venezuela and Guyana and at the mouth of the Amazon.

The coast in these regions is unusual in appearance. From a distance the mangrove swamp seems to merge with the green of the coastal forest, but at closer quarters an extra-

Above, left
mangrove trees,
with their strange
exposed roots, at
high tide and
right at low tide

ordinary landscape is revealed. The forest and the sea meet on the shore in an eternal battle which has lasted many thousands of years. Often the forest gains ground and the water flows round the trees, exerting pressure on the trunks, roots, boles and branches, and yet they continue to grow. Then suddenly a hurricane or typhoon will sweep the area, flattening parts of the forest. Once calm returns, however, the forest starts to spread again. The swamp vegetation comprises mainly plants of the *Rhizophora* genus (the name means root-bearing) and other allied species.

The principal plant found in the swamps on the coast of Florida and the Mexican Gulf is the red mangrove (*Rhizophora mangle*), a very insistent and aggressive tree. When they were first seen by a doctor on board Christopher Columbus's ship he described them as being 'so dense that even a rabbit could hardly have passed through between them.'

Like Columbus the red mangrove is a great traveller and the American mangrove is thought to come originally from the west coast of Africa. This is some distance, but the recent *Ra* expedition proved that it could have been

possible for it to have been brought to America by the sea current.

The red mangrove propagates rapidly. Just by following the development of one plant it is possible to illustrate how vast mangrove forests can grow. The flowers of the mangrove are formed similarly to those of any other plant, the yellow flowers being stellate, 2 to 3 cm in diameter, and blooming in spring. Nor is there anything remarkable about the fruit, at least initially. But then something strange happens: while the fruit is still on the tree a firm green root grows gradually downwards, like a sort of bean pod. Towards the end of August or beginning of September the fruits ripen and are ready to fall from the tree. By then a miniature tree has begun to form, complete with roots. This is a classic example of adaptation to the environment. The seeds of trees generally germinate in the ground but the coastal soil contains too much salt for this to happen. The mangrove therefore retains its fruit until the seeds have germinated and are ready to grow.

By the time they fall to the ground they are ready to take root and, if not carried away from the parent tree by the tides or a storm, they will

Above, left the small flower of the yellow water-lily

Above, right the white water-lily has roots extending to the bed of the water on which it grows

Left mushrooms of the genus *Omphalia*, found only on waterlogged ground

Right cotton grass, which comes originally from Alpine marshlands. One species has been cultivated and is grown in gardens

Above the lotus flower is one of the oldest aquatic plants. It came originally from Egypt and Asia Minor but is now found throughout the world

grow under it within a short space of time, adding to the already dense forest. Others might be carried for hundreds or even thousands of miles by the current before they are finally washed up on some distant shore. All they need then are a few days of calm to enable them to establish their roots and start a new forest.

Once the plants are about two years old they begin to develop roots which grow out to the side in an arc and establish themselves in the ground some way from the trunk, forming a support for the tree. These roots serve various purposes. They anchor the plant to the muddy ground, so that it can withstand the waves, tides and winds. They keep the trunk above the water and, at the same time, supply it with the liquid it requires. Furthermore they are exposed to the air and can absorb oxygen which the plant would not otherwise be able to obtain from the muddy soil.

As the roots grow they protect the trees from the force of the waves and tides. Mud and debris accumulate round them, providing a more stable foundation for the plants and gradually reclaiming land from the sea, which is slowly forced into retreat. Although storms and hurricanes may flatten stretches of the forest and return the land temporarily to the sea, it has been estimated that over the last forty years the mangrove forests have usurped about

1,500 acres of coastal shallows in certain parts of Florida, creating impenetrable swamps.

It must not, however, be forgotten that as well as these sea-swamps there are also numerous freshwater marshes of considerable interest. In some cases these may be the inland reaches of sea-marshes where the sea-water has lost its salinity, but the majority of freshwater marshes have never contained any salt. They may develop round a pool, river or lake or, if the climatic conditions are right, form in complete isolation, covering vast tracts of flat country.

The typical aquatic environment, around which marshes form, might be a small lake, where there is, of course, very little wave action, or a larger expanse of water which nevertheless contains fairly extensive shallows and affords sufficient protection for the vegetation. The type of lake is unimportant, though marshes do tend to form less readily in an alluvial environment as the silt which collects may prevent the growth of marsh vegetation.

The vegetation specific to the marsh environment comprises plants which prefer humid conditions and grow either wholly or partially submersed or floating on the water surface. Organic deposits of humus from dead plants slowly raise the level of the marsh bed and, if the basin is fairly small, this will also result in a rise in the water level, causing the marsh to overflow slowly on to surrounding land.

There is a very varied plant community of bog mosses (*Sphagnum*), reeds, cat's tails, sagittaria, water-lilies, etc. Each species lives at a particular depth and the plants tend to grow in concentric bands extending out from the centre of the marsh to the edges. Some plants, like the bog mosses, salvinia, water-ferns, duckweed etc., float on the surface, some live completely under the water, while others, such as water-lilies, extend their roots to the mud bed, their leaves floating on the surface of the water.

The floating plants grow in clusters, with those which are alive pushing up to the top and burying the dead ones underneath them. These clusters are constantly spreading, not just because the plants grow rapidly but also because they amass various sorts of organic debris. In time they can become sufficiently dense to support a fairly rich growth of reeds, bushes and even trees. Often they are solid enough to walk on, though the water underfoot will seep through as weight is applied.

Their surface is a veritable microcosm of life – bog mosses, brightly coloured fungi of all shapes, sundews with their iridescent tentacles and aquatic flora and plants of all types.

This continual accumulation of sediment gradually fills in the basin. This, therefore, represents a good illustration of the constant evolution of the marsh environment. To begin with it is no more than a pool of water where any vegetation is submerged. Then emergent aquatic plants, like the reeds, begin to appear and finally it becomes a water-saturated ground, characterized by a vegetation of sedges (*Carex*). Eventually trees such as willow, alders and poplars may begin to grow in the humid environment. By this point the area has undergone a complete transformation and the ground is now solid enough to support these broad-leafed tree species.

All this happens slowly and gradually and the various stages in this progression do not follow one upon the other in strict succession. The vegetation from one phase can coexist quite happily with that from subsequent phases, resulting in a fairly diverse community of plants which have adapted to the marsh environment and have established themselves in the zone which best suits their requirements, usually determined by depth.

Aquatic plants in the true sense of the term cover the organic slime of the bed and grow completely submerged in the water. These include tape-grasses (*Vallisneria*), a perennial plant with a short rhizome which anchors it in the ground and long ribbon-like leaves, making it somewhat reminiscent of *Posidonia oceanica*. The Canadian water-weed (*Elodea canadensis*) comes originally from North America but is also found widely in stagnant or slow-flowing water in Europe. It is commonly known as the water-weed because of the rapidity with which it can infest an area. A smooth, shiny plant with a long, thin, branched stalk and small ovoid leaves, it is sometimes used in aquaria as an ornamental plant. Ducks and swans are extremely fond of it. Another plant similar in

Below a common water-fern is the floating salvinia, the leaves of which are grouped in pairs

27

Above pondweeds attach themselves to the bed by large rhizomes and long stalks

appearance to the *Elodea* is the water-milfoil (*Myriophyllum verticillatum*), but its leaves are like a fine comb.

There are also numerous species that have roots anchored in the marsh bed but leaves floating on the surface and many others not anchored at all but simply floating on the surface. These include certain carnivorous plants, among them the *Utricularia*, which grows mainly in tropical regions but is also found in temperate zones.

To biologists the most interesting aspect of this floating plant is its leaves, which might be mistaken for roots by a layman, as they resemble long, entwined branches, entirely submersed and forking out in all directions. Closer examination will, however, reveal curious leaves growing on these branches, no more than small, bladder-like sacs. But these sacs are, in fact, lethal traps for the innumerable tiny creatures which inhabit stagnant waters. The traps have a sort of flap which opens inwards; once the animal is inside it cannot escape because

the flap springs shut and will not re-open outwards as it is larger than the entrance it seals off. The trap is lined inside with cells secreting enzymes which digest the prey and the ingenuity of the whole device is completed by a gas inside the trap which has a higher pressure than the water outside. This keeps the door firmly closed and prevents water from entering as the creature hurls itself around inside in a frantic effort to escape.

One of the best known marsh carnivores is the *Dionaea muscipula*, which is found only in Carolina. It was first discovered in about 1750 by Arthur Dobbs, Governor of North Carolina. Linnaeus, the Swedish botanist, was so amazed by the plant that he called it '*miraculum naturae*', a miracle of nature. Indeed, these plants use an ingenious mechanism to capture their prey: the ends of their leaves have two facing lobes in a circle along the veins; the ends of the lobes are hooked and on the centre of each are three tiny but highly sensitive hairs. If an insect brushes against these hairs the trap will spring shut, with the lobes closing fast.

Found throughout the world is the insectivorous sundew (*Drosera*), of which there are about a hundred different species. They generally grow in ground saturated with water and lacking nutrients. They are small plants with a rosette of tiny leaves, at the end of which is a fairly large round lobe (in some species this lobe can be long and thin like a thread). The whole of the upper surface of the lobe is covered with long hairs which end in a pin-head shape. This head is permanently covered with a tiny drop of liquid, often reddish in colour, which reflects the light and makes the leaf shine from afar. The shiny droplets contain a sticky liquid and when insects attracted by the light land on the leaves they are trapped. As they try to free themselves they are bound to touch other tentacles and become even more entangled. Once the prey is captured, the tentacles secrete digestive enzymes and thus absorb nutrients from the insect. All that finally remains of it is the empty shell.

Another carnivorous plant found fairly frequently in this type of environment is the *Aldrovando*, small and sappy and not more than 15 cm long. It is almost transparent and lives suspended in the water, but again it is the leaves which are of interest. They, too, act as a trap which closes when stimuli are received by hairs inside it. Aquatic plants found in fresh-

water marshes in temperate regions include the pondweeds (*Potamogeton*), knot grass (*Polygonum*), which is characterised by a panicle of pink flowers, and frog-bit (*Hydrocharis morsus-ranae*), which has small white flowers.

There are, of course, other, more impressive flowering plants, such as the water-lily with its large, circular leaves that float on the surface. This plant can be very sensitive to changes in the ambient temperature, humidity and light and its flowers will open and close rapidly. An extremely attractive variety is the *Nymphaea alba*, which flowers from April to August. The stalk is long enough to allow the flowers to bloom on the surface and has longitudinal air passages running through it; these lead to the roots embedded in the mud and supply the submerged parts of the plant with oxygen. The fine flowers are large and white and have a delicate perfume.

Nuphar luteum is similar in appearance to the *Nymphaea* and is also a member of the Nymphaeaceae family, but its flowers are quite different, being smaller and yellow in colour. They have a characteristic smell of alcohol which attracts insects.

There are numerous tropical species of water-lily. Their flowers display a wide range of colour and they are often grown for ornamental purposes. One variety from equatorial America, the *Victoria regia*, is, however, known not so much for the beauty of its flowers but more for the size and shape of its leaves, which are circular and have a diameter of 1.5 to 2 m. Their edges curve upwards, somewhat like a boat, and because of their size and concave shape they can support quite considerable weights. They are protected against aquatic creatures by sharp little spines in the veins on the underside.

Another member of the water-lily family, which originates from Egypt and Asia Minor and was introduced into Europe as an ornamental plant, is the lotus (*Nelumbo nucifera*) which has pink or scarlet flowers. The species, now spread to Asia and America, produces an interesting fruit which resembles a watering-

Above a hippopotamus swimming in a pool in Kenya, flanked by papyrus. Feeding mostly at night, the hippopotamus never wanders very far from water

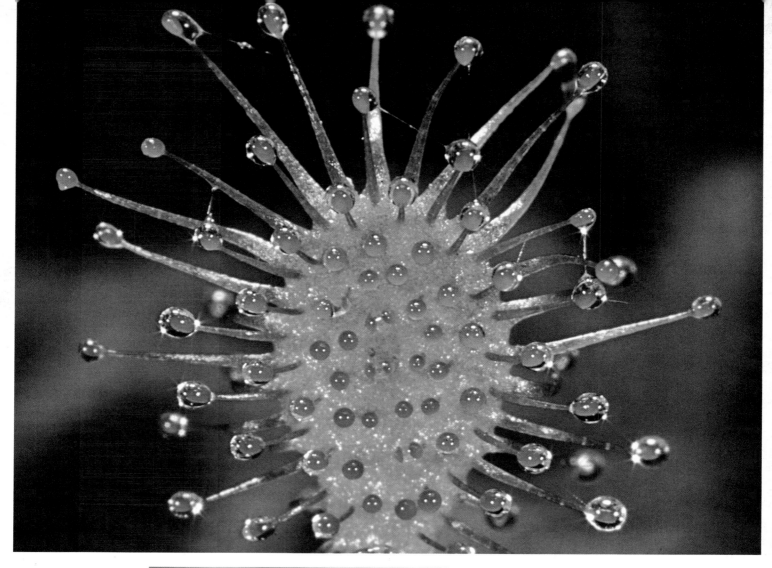

Above the insectivorous *Drosera* are typical wetland plants. Here is a close-up of a head of the plant, while at right is an insect which has just been trapped by the sticky tentacles

can rose in that its upper section is pitted with large holes containing the seeds, which are themselves known as Egyptian beans. There is also a native American species, the water chinquapin (*N. luteum*), with yellow flowers.

The water-chestnut (*Trapa natans*) is another large floating plant. Its leaves are fan-shaped, grouped together in the form of rosettes, and can completely cover the surface of vast expanses of marsh and stagnant water. It is found in some lakes and marshes in Northern Italy, Tuscany and Apulia. The fruits bear a slight resemblance to chestnuts and can be eaten in the same way, namely boiled or roasted.

From a distance this floating vegetation can give marshes and stretches of water the appearance of grass-covered fields. A great many species of plant contribute to this vegetation, including in particular those of the duckweed (*Lemna*) and water-fern families.

Duckweeds are found widely in many areas of marsh and stagnant water in both temperate and tropical climates. A common variety is the *Lemna minor*, which is known as the lesser

duckweed or water-lentil. It has tiny round leaves from which roots grow down directly into the water. These leaves tend to separate easily and the plant reproduces thus by agamogenesis, or asexual reproduction. A related species, the greater duckweed (*L. polyrrhiza*), has larger leaves and grows in Northern Italy and Sardinia.

The water-fern family includes the *Salvinia natans*, which is easily recognisable from its distinctive appearance. Its leaves are grouped in pairs and covered in large papilla, which make them look like an ox's tongue. Also found in Europe is the *Salvinia rotundifolia*, which was introduced from Central and South America and has become particularly established in Spain. Its leaves are larger and more rounded than those of *S. natans* and will soon spread to cover the entire surface of any stretch of water in which they grow.

A species of fern found in the stagnant waters of the Po valley, Italy, is the *Azolla caroliniana*, which comes originally from America. It has small, closely bunched leaves with a lobe on which blue algae and bacteria grow. The *Marsilea quadrifolia* is another variety found widely in Europe and is generally known as the water- or marsh-quadrifoliate or trifoliate.

The vegetation of the shallow waters and marsh edges is also of a fairly characteristic type. Here the plant community consists mainly of a varied range of emergent aquatics. The *Sagittaria sagittifolia*, commonly known as the arrowhead, is unusual in that it has leaves of three entirely different shapes. Those under water are long and ribbon-like, while the floating leaves are round or heart-shaped and the emergent ones are like an arrowhead, giving the name to the plant.

Other emergent plants found commonly in marsh environments are the water-plantain (*Alisma plantago acquatica*), the horsetail (*Equisetum palustre*), the flowering rush (*Butomus umbellatus*), the water-violet (*Hottonia palustris*), which has star-shaped flowers, and the water forget-me-not (*Myosotis palustris*). By far the most beautiful, however, is the yellow flag (*Iris pseudacorus*) which is a fairly common marsh

Above the Venus fly-trap is a carnivorous plant found on the edges of marshland in Carolina

plant in southern Europe and which also grows in ditches and along canal banks. The flowers are yellow and similar to those of Italy's Florentine lily.

It is common for plants living on the edge of marshes to be found growing in bands. The outer bands generally consist of cat's-tails (*Typha latifolia* and *T. angustifolia*) with their long thin leaves and characteristic female flowers like a fairly long brown panicle round the top of the stalk. Further in towards the centre are the marsh reeds (*Phragmites communis*). These are anchored to the bottom by means of a long rhizome which puts out trailing or floating stolons. There are almost always clumps of reeds in the marsh. Their feathery flowers are purple to begin with, turning to pale-yellow, and even the slightest breath of wind causes them to sway gently.

The band of rushes is found still further towards the water. It comprises the marsh rush (*Scirpus lacuster* and *S. maritimus*), which is often found in pools and coastal marshes, and the *Juncus conglomeratus*. The last of these is often allied with the yellow flag and at one time the pith used to be extracted from it in a long white thread and used as a taper for lighting lamps. Beyond this band of rushes come the water-lilies.

Another interesting plant living on the edge of expanses of freshwater is the papyrus (*Cyperus papyrus*). It is more common in Africa than in Europe, where it is found only on the banks of the River Ciane in Sicily. It isn't known whether the Sicilian variety is the relic of an ancient and much larger natural colony of papyrus or whether, as is more likely, it was introduced during early Greek or Arabian times.

Some marshes are seasonal and form only after river floods or heavy rainfall. For example, the Amazon floods regularly, producing what has been described as a semi-submersed world where the vegetation and water are engaged in an eternal battle, advancing and retreating with the flood seasons. The tributaries are swollen by torrential rains from March to July in the north and from October to January in the south, and flooding extends as much as 85 km into the forest.

In order to survive, the vegetation of the region has to adapt to this semi-aquatic environ-

Facing page, top an Alpine marsh, lush with vegetation

Bottom a scene in the Everglades in Florida, where the seasonal changes can have a drastic effect on the animal life of some areas

Below a plant found fairly commonly on the periphery of a marsh is the cat's tail, distinguished by its long thin leaves

Above dawn over Lake Baringo in the Rift Valley, Kenya

ment and does well on the rich silt left by the floods. Water-ferns float on the surface and absorb nutrients through their leaves, but as a rule the flowers adopt a different solution in that they no longer grow in the ground but attach themselves like epiphytes to the branches of trees. There they absorb sufficient moisture for their needs from the atmosphere and from rainwater. By this and other similar devices the plant community is able to withstand repeated onslaughts from the water. During the floods the trees temporarily suffocate, due to insufficient oxygen in the roots, and lose their leaves, with the result that they appear like skeletons on the mud landscape. It is only when the waters recede that the plants begin to flourish again but natural regeneration often takes its time.

Other marshes form on flat ground where the rainwater does not drain away but remains in pools on the surface of the earth. Some of these are seasonal marshes, such as those in Venezuela, which evaporate during the dry season. Certain parts of the Everglades also dry up in particular seasons and the animals which inhabit the water are forced to adapt to these conditions in order to survive until the rains begin again. In the tundra regions the opposite happens: the land is marsh during the summer season but in winter is completely covered in snow and ice.

Marshes are also found in mountainous regions as well as in flat, low-lying areas. Sometimes high ground may be so flat or the geographical structure such that the water from the rain or from the melting snows does not drain away and a small marsh is formed. Often mountain marshes develop between glacial moraine deposits or round a tarn which has formed because of the impervious nature of the bedrock. In the Alps, for example, there are numerous patches of brightly coloured sphagnum mosses. The special vegetation of these areas in some ways resembles that of the tundra because of the cold climate, as evidenced by the dwarf willow and cotton-grass, found both here and in bogs and marshes in Scandinavia and Finland.

Wetland habitats and their characteristic plants

MARSH

Formed on inorganic silt or clay soils with water level during the summer at or near the surface. Most typical plants are rushes:

Compact rush (*Juncus conglomeratus*)

Hard rush (*J. inflexus*)

Jointed rush (*J. articulatus*)

Sharp-flowered rush (*J. acutiflorus*)

Another characteristic plant is the Tufted hair grass (*Deschampsis cespitosa*). Marsh vegetation is often lush and includes many attractive species such as:

Marsh marigold (*Caltha palustris*)

Yellow flag iris (*Iris pseudocorus*)

Water forget-me-not (*Myosotis scorpioides*)

Marsh orchid (*Dactylorchis*).

FEN

Wetland in which the organic soil is either alkaline or neutral with a highly characteristic vegetation often dominated by:

Saw sedge (*Cladium mariscus*) or Purple small reed (*Calmagrostis epigejos*)

Uncommon plants include:

Fen orchid (*Liparis loeselii*)

Fen bedstraw (*Galium uliginosum*)

Milk parsley (*Peucedanum palustre*)

If left undisturbed, the vegetation often gradually changes into alder 'carr' then alderwood dominated by the

Alder (*Alnus glutmosa*)

Common buckthorn (*Rhamnus cathartica*)

Alder buckthorn (*Frangula alnus*).

SWAMP

A marsh in which the summer water level is above the surface. This zone is most often dominated by tall plants like:

Reed (*Phragmitis communis*)

Great reedmace (*Typha latifolia*)

True Bulrush (*Schoenoplectus lacustris*)

Other notable plants are the bur-reeds (*Sparganium*) with conspicuous spiky fruits in late summer and the beautiful flowering rush (*Butomus umbellatus*) with its inch-wide rose-pink petals. At the edge of the water one can find the amphibious persicaria (*Polygonum amphibium*) with its elongated leaves floating on the surface.

BOG

A wetland consisting of wet acid peat. Dominated by various species of *Sphagnum* moss. Its most characteristic higher plant is Cotton grass or Bog cotton (*Eriophorum angustifolium*) which whitens the bogs in early early summer when the cottony threads of the fruit appear.

Other plants include:

Bog Asphodel (*Narthecium ossifragum*)

Bog Pimpernel (*Anagallis tenella*)

Bog orchid (*Malaxis paludosa*) also insectivorous plants like the Butterworts (*Pinguicula*) and the Sundews (*Drosera*).

Chapter Two

The Marsh Microcosm

*In one day the organic material produced
in the marsh environment is up to fifty times greater
than that of grassland and mountain forests and up to eight
times greater than that of cultivated or tropical fields. This rich production
of foodstuffs provides an important substrate for prolific
animal life and in this chapter, the authors describe the complete
food-chain to be found in marshlands ranging upwards
from unicellular algae to predatory animals.*

Facing page
A cloud of mosquitoes rise above their marshland
breeding-ground. Some seventy species of mosquito are known to
transmit the micro-organism that causes malaria

Apart from a few exceptions, such as the peat bog, marshes have an abundant growth of vegetation. It has been calculated that in one day the primary production of the marsh environment (i.e. the organic material produced by plants simply from air, water, solar energy and chemical elements) can be up to fifty times greater than that of grassland or mountain forests and three to eight times that of cultivated fields or tropical forests. Only sugar-cane cultivation can compare with marsh, lagoon or brackish water vegetation in this respect.

This rich production of organic vegetable matter provides an important substrate for the prolific animal life. A wide range of foods, from the unicellular algae and phytoplankton and the like through to the more developed plant species, is available to the vegetarian animal community (the primary consumers). They in turn may represent a source of food for predator animals, thus establishing a fairly complex food-chain.

This type of environment fosters the development of animal life and it has played a major role in evolution. Life began at the time when the Earth's surface was covered with vast expanses of marshland. Mud lagoons already existed along the ocean shores in the Devonian age and it was during this period that shellfish and large crustaceans left the sea, dragged themselves up on to the soft, slippery mud and established a home in the fern swamplands. Within a few million years, a relatively short time in geological terms, the marshes had become the habitat of thousands of animal species.

From fossils which have been found it is possible to obtain a picture, sometimes very rough and sometimes very precise, of the strange creatures which lived in this environment, such as the gigantic arthropod species resembling scorpions but generally about 3 m long. These were followed by vertebrates: first of all fish and then, towards the end of the initial era, amphibians. Fish with fringed fins attached to strange peduncles evolved into fish-like creatures which retained their dorsal fin but had replaced the rest by webbed feet. These early amphibians were like huge salamanders inhabiting a jungle of aquatic vegetation consisting of giant ferns and horse-tails. They were joined by fearsome arthropods such as carnivorous dragonflies, huge millipedes and giant spiders.

Huge bugs attached themselves to the stalks of aquatic plants and tree trunks, sucking nourishment from the sap. Clouds of locusts and mantises and hordes of beetles and crickets the size of pumpkins swarmed the marshes, terrifying the smaller inhabitants with their loud buzzing. These small creatures would then be beset by a frantic panic and thus attract the attention of the monsters to which they would eventually fall victim.

Fossils show that in the Carboniferous age the marshes were inhabited by identical insects to those which now live not only in the marshes but also on dry land. The only difference is that they have now diminished in size. We no longer find huge prehistoric dragonflies with a wing-span of 70 cm, but the basic shape of the creature has not altered at all. This shows a strength and resistance to changes in the environment not

Below left and right respectively: mosquito larvae and pupae

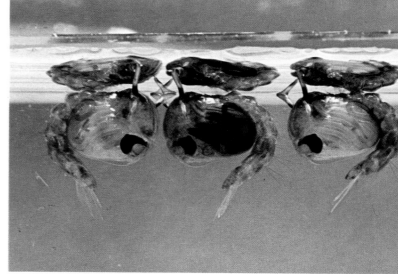

exhibited by any other animal. In fact species from later ages which seemed to represent the ultimate in strength and power, such as the huge dinosaurs inhabiting the marsh during the second epoch, have become completely extinct. Only fossilised remains bear witness to the existence of animals like the varanosaurus, sphenodon, dimetrodon and triceratops.

Then there was the huge brontosaurus, over 20 m long and weighing more than 40 tons. It lived only in water and indeed was unable to haul itself on to solid ground without collapsing under its own tremendous weight. These creatures tended to wallow in mud, which prevented them from being molested by insects. The tyrannosaurus, though not quite as large as the brontosaurus, was another huge monster, with a disproportionately large head containing rows of razor-sharp teeth up to 20 cm long. Although undoubtedly the most fearsome creature ever found on land, it did not survive. The vast marshes receded to within smaller confines and new animal species appeared – reptiles, birds and mammals. Only the insects managed to survive in their original form.

These marsh environments have been the scene of many changes throughout the various phases of evolution and today they are still a focus for animal life. The prime reason for this is the rich production of vegetation mentioned above.

A complex food-chain begins with the phytoplankton, unicellular organisms which breed prolifically in the marsh environment. These include cyanophyceae, diatoms and chlorophyceae. They grow well because of the abundance of mineral salts dissolved in the water and because of the shallowness of the water itself. For these reasons there is a considerable amount of light in the water and this facilitates chlorophyll photosynthesis. Consequently some of the unicellular algae are rich in energy-giving and nutrient elements. It is believed that some species of chlorella, unicellular fresh-water algae, contain 50 per cent protein, 20 per cent fats, 20 per cent sugars and 10 per cent mineral salts, which means they are six times more rich in protein than rice and contain fifty times more vitamin A than milk.

These phytoplankton are consumed directly by the microscopic animals known as the zooplankton (the larvae of crustaceans, molluscs, copepods etc.). The zooplankton themselves provide food for the larger animals and

so on up to the predator birds and mammals. On the other hand, some of the larger animals, such as the crustaceans, molluscs, insects and even some birds and mammals, feed directly on much larger vegetable matter than zooplankton. This creates a whole series of fairly complex interrelationships between the animal and the plant world which will be dealt with as we look at the various inhabitants of the marsh environment.

The marsh does, in fact, represent a classic example of an 'ecosystem', i.e. a self-contained living system. This starts, as we have said, with the 'producers', the phytoplankton and larger plants, some species of which have been described briefly in the preceding chapter.

The second group is that of the 'consumers', which in their turn can be subdivided into three categories: there are the primary consumers which feed directly on the producers, namely the zooplankton and larger animals like the crustaceans (shrimps, daphnia etc.), the gastropod molluscs which live in aquatic vegetation (snails and planorbis), the phytophagic insects, vegetarian fish and birds (coot, duck and moorhen) and lastly a few mammals (such as the muskrat).

The next category is that of secondary consumers, those which feed on herbivorous animals. They include the coleoptera (for instance the water-beetle), the majority of dragonflies, carnivorous fish such as the carp, the frogs and toads and the insectivorous and fish-eating birds like the grebe and heron.

The third group of consumers comprises those which feed on animals in the second

Below pond snails, among the many gastropods found throughout the world in freshwater or very damp environments

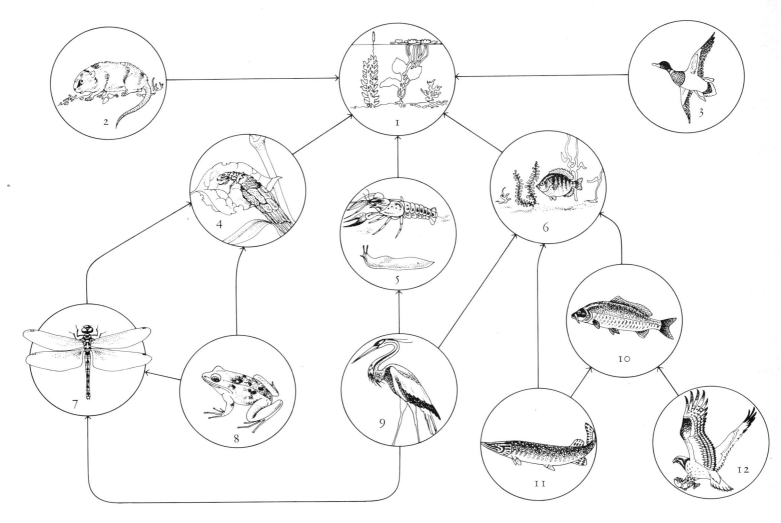

Above the marsh
ecosystem; an
illustration of the
food chain
1 phytoplankton
  and higher plants
2 musk rat
3 duck
4 plant-eating
  insects
5 crustaceans and
  molluscs
6 plant-eating fish
7 dragonfly
8 frog
9 heron
10 carnivorous
  fish
11 pike
12 osprey

group, the carnivores. They are fairly small in number and include the pike, which lives on young perch, and the marsh harrier, which steals from the nests of gulls and terns.

After the producers and the consumers come the 'waste decomposers' to complete the cycle. They consume the remains of all the other plants and animals and process them, turning them into minerals. The main species in question are the bacteria and fungi.

It must be made clear, however, that the above scheme is concerned only with the relationships between animals in the food-chain. These relationships are rendered more complex by the fact that every animal can belong simultaneously to more than one of the above groups. They can be primary and secondary and tertiary consumers, depending on the season or simply on what they can capture to eat. It is consequently impossible to find an absolute definition for the term 'prey' since any marsh creature may be both prey and predator.

Prey can, therefore, be defined only in terms of particular species, i.e. it is possible to say that one particular animal is the prey of a certain other species. For example, certain types of birds seem to live on insects; they are the staple diet of small passerine birds, reed warblers and green marsh linnets, and some non-aquatic birds, such as the swallow, will make incursions into the marsh in search of insects.

The favourite prey of the insectivorous marsh birds is the dragonfly. This is due to the fact that its size enables it to be seen from some distance away and also that many species, especially those in the suborder of the zygoptera, fly fairly slowly and awkwardly. They make an easy catch for birds such as the gull and tern, which can attain a good speed in the air. The dragonfly larvae are carnivorous aquatic creatures which represent a constant source of danger for the smaller inhabitants of the underwater regions. But these larvae are themselves preyed upon by fish while they dwell in the water and are later a favourite food of birds as they emerge on the surface on reaching adulthood. At this stage they are particularly vulnerable and are even in

danger from a number of birds which would not normally regard them as food, e.g. the grebe, water rail and moorhen.

The frog is also fond of the dragonfly, but it in turn, however well camouflaged, may fall victim to other predators. Often its incessant croaking betrays its presence and the frog is therefore familiar with the danger and always on the alert. At the slightest strange sound it is ready to dive. It has to be taken by surprise by a stealthy hunter such as the heron, which is able to remain perfectly still until its presence is forgotten by the frog. As soon as the latter re-appears on the surface the heron's beak spears it like a harpoon and devours the prey for which it has waited so patiently. These brief examples give some idea of the complexity of the relationships between the various inhabitants of the marsh. Before going on to discuss these in more detail is is worth saying a few words about some of the marsh species.

The marsh is basically an aquatic environment and it would seem appropriate to begin with an outline of those creatures which live in the water. They are often small, quiet, inconspicuous creatures, unlikely to be spotted by an untrained or casual observer.

From a distance the algae, which cover the bottoms of certain lagoons and salt or brackish coastal pools and are left exposed at low tide, appear like a lifeless green desert, but a closer inspection will show just how false this impression is. These algae are the home of tiny creatures such as bivalve molluscs which lie with their valves tightly closed waiting for the water level to rise again. Tiny shrimps force a path through the vegetation in search of water. These are generally grey shrimps, like those found on the sea shore. They have adapted to the environment by increasing their normal sea density when they are in brackish pools. The larger crabs make their way carefully over the algae. Another creature found in brackish water is the marsh snail (*Limnea palustris*) which is similar in appearance to the freshwater variety. It has a long spiral-shaped shell. If suddenly surprised by a drop in water level it will withdraw inside this shell and secrete a viscous substance which

Above frog and dragonfly enact an everyday drama of the swamp

41

hardens on contact with the air. This seals the shell and the gastropod can retain the minute amount of moisture required for it to stay alive. Like other snail species, it is able to crawl along under the surface with only the thinnest film of liquid separating it from the air. In this position it can amass any plant fragments that have fallen on to the surface of the water.

Lagoons and brackish marshes are rich in fish; some come in from the sea at certain times of the year, while others breed there as prolifically as in a hatchery. The sort of fish found in these waters include the brill (*Bothus*), the sole (*Solea*), the sea bream (*Dentex dentex* and *Oblada melanura*), the red mullet (*Mullus barbatus* and *M. surmuletus*), the sardine (*Sardina pilchardus*), the gunnard (*Trigla*), the anchovy (*Engraulis encrasicholus*), the common mackerel

(*Scomber scomber*), the salpa (*Salpa*), the goby (*Gobius*) and the atherine (*Atherina mochon*). Some species of fish are truly migratory in nature. They come into the lagoon at a specific time and remain for one or two years as they grow.

Of the fish which live in the brackish marshes of the Mediterranean there is one which is of no value to fishermen but is of interest to naturalists. This is the pipefish (*Syngnathus acus*). It is of the same family as the sea-horse (*Cavalluccio marino*), although it does not have the latter's unusual shape. It is known as the pipefish because of its long body, to which the dorsal fin seems to give added length, making it difficult to distinguish among the water vegetation. The female lays her eggs in a sac in the male's abdomen. He broods for several weeks without

Below Sympetrum sanguineum, one of the most beautiful marshland species of dragonflies

eating and only when the young are hatched and able to swim does he start eating again. He prefers copepods or shrimps but will also eat certain molluscs.

The brackish marshes, lagoons and salt and brackish coastal pools are an ideal breeding-ground for molluscs and crustaceans. The muddy bed is full of bivalve molluscs such as those of the Veneridae and Cardiidae families, and a study conducted in a brackish marsh in Massachusetts revealed that an area of mud 10 cm square could contain thirty different species.

Brackish waters such as the Thau basin in the south of France are a breeding-ground for mussels, oysters and other molluscs, among them the *Solen vagina, Murex trunculus, Arca diluvii* and *Venus verrucosa*, as well as crustaceans

Below detail of a dragonfly larva showing its predacious mouth

Bottom the head of a dragonfly with characteristic prominent, bulbous eyes

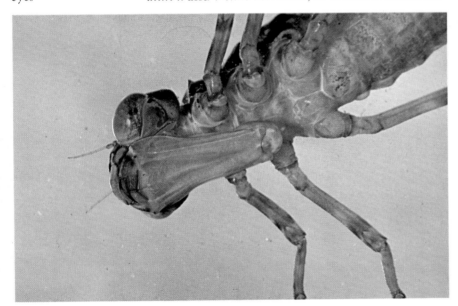

such as the lobster (*Crangon*) and crab (*Carcinus maenas*). It must also be remembered that many crustaceans thought of as sea-dwellers may spend some time in brackish waters and, in certain cases, breed there.

Inland freshwater marshes also have a rich variety of animal life, which again is revealed only on close observation. The surface of a marsh will often look like a field with a luxuriant undergrowth. The floating plants hide those underneath from view and most of the animal inhabitants are too small to be seen. There are the microscopic Protozoa, for example, which include the amoebae. These creatures feed in an unusual way in that they are made up of one large cell and, on finding a particle of food, they approach and envelope it in protoplasm. They then digest it slowly through the cell membranes.

One of the most common infusorians (organisms found in infusions of organic substances), is the paramecium, which moves by means of its cilia. These creatures are also uni-cellular and this cell, unlike those which form part of more complex organisms, has a certain individuality. It combines all the vital processes which take place in a living organism, such as feeding, digestion, respiration and reproduction. It has, however, only a short life, lasting from a few hours to one or two days, and is a favourite food of all the smaller marsh creatures, young fish and insect larvae.

There is also an abundance of creatures which, though not microscopic, are very small indeed. These include copepods of the *Cyclops* genus; cyprids, tiny crustaceans with a bivalve shell protecting the body; and the water-flea, *Daphnia cladoceri*. In the late spring it is common to find swarms of these minuscule creatures at the edges of the marsh where the water is shallower and the vegetation less dense, giving the impression that the water itself is alive.

Other inhabitants include various species of worms and leeches, like the *Haemopsis sanguisuga* or *Hirudo medicinalis*, which though not as big as the tropical varieties can be 10–15 cm or more in length.

One member of the annelid family worthy of special mention is the *Tubifex tubifex*, a small pink worm which lives in and obtains its nourishment from the mud. This amorphous substance, which feeds by processing and assimilating the mud, does, in fact, contain the elements the worm requires for survival. It has a smooth

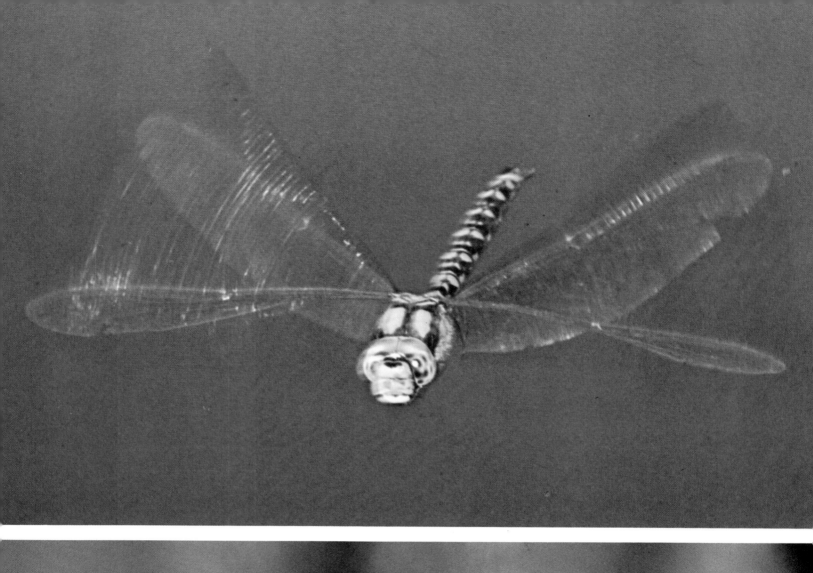

skin that enables it to burrow into the ground and slide with ease through subterranean passages. The passages, incidentally, help to aerate the marsh bed and thus aid the growth of marsh vegetation.

The most characteristic marsh annelids are the leeches, which require water or at least a certain humidity in order to survive. They can swim very quickly, weaving through the water on strong muscles. Their body is very flexible and, in the case of the more common species, has a sucker at either end. It is not possible to distinguish at a glance the front from the back. In actual fact the rear sucker is used solely as a means of adhesion while the front one has three tiny, sharp teeth which it uses to puncture the skin of the victim. By alternately contracting and relaxing the pharynx muscles it draws blood from the victim and stores it in the small sacs which run the length of its body. The blood is impregnated with a special substance to prevent it from clotting and is then slowly digested by the creature.

Molluscs may not be as prolific as in brackish waters, but freshwater marshes still contain considerable numbers. They include *Unio* and *Anodonta* (genera of the Lamellibrancha class) and, more especially, *Limnea* and *Planorbis* genera of the Gastropoda.

The pond snail (*Limnea stagnalis*) is a gastropod which breathes through lungs and is consequently obliged to surface from time to time in order to take in air. Its lungs have a capacity of $1-1.5$ cm^3, which means that if human beings had the equivalent proportional capacity they would be able to inhale fifteen litres of air instead of the normal five and a half. The pond snail moves along just under the surface, adhering to the thin film between air and water. In this position it can expel used air and then fill its lungs with a fresh supply, before sinking into the water again.

Insects constitute a fairly large proportion of all marsh inhabitants. The majority live in the water only while they are in the chrysalis and pupa stages, but some, such as the water-boatman, water-scorpion and water-beetle, continue to live in the water even after reaching maturity. One common variety of water-beetle, the *Dytiscus marginalis*, passes its entire life in water. In fact no other insect appears better adapted to an aquatic environment than

Above dragonflies (*Nehalennia speciosa*) in the act of mating on a branch

Facing page, top a dragonfly of the *Aeschna* species in flight

Bottom a male *Coneagrion puella* dragonfly devouring a mosquito

this beetle, with its streamlined, boat-shaped body 3–5 cm in length. It is brown with green tinges and has a yellow-ocre stripe along the elytra, or front wings. It is perfectly at home in water because it is able to secrete a fatty substance which keeps its body dry and because it can remain submerged for long periods and still breathe from a reserve of air collected under the elytra. Instinct dictates to the water-beetle how to use this reserve of air, always leaving it enough to reach the surface when the supply is exhausted. Its rear legs have long, thick bristles which can be used like oars, allowing the beetle to move more quickly and freely through the water than it can on its rare flights.

The adult water-beetle is capable of attacking and devouring larger aquatic creatures, including even sizable newts and frogs. Even as larvae they exhibit considerable independence and ferocity. The larva has two strong pincers, each of which has a tiny duct running down it to the pharynx. When any likely prey approaches it prepares these pincers for action, then with lightning speed clamps its jaw round the victim and paralyses it by injecting a poison through its mandible channels; it then injects powerful digestive juices which predigest the tissue and penetrate the body, reducing the creature to a

watery mush. The beetle's pharynx then begins to work in reverse, slowly sucking up the food that would otherwise have been too much for the mouth to handle. As if anxious not to soil its own territory, the larva disposes of its excrement outside the water by surfacing and hurling it on to the bank or some nearby plant.

This method of feeding is not by any means unique to the water-beetle. A number of insects use a toxic secretion to capture their prey and there is one marsh dweller which has many times the capacity of the water-beetle in this respect. This is the giant water-bug, of the Belostomatidae family, which is not found in Europe but only in North and South America. This insect holds its victim with its front legs, pierces the skin or shell of the other insect, fish or frog with its proboscis and proceeds to inject chemicals which turn the muscles, intestines and internal organs into a liquid. The water-bug then ingests these juices, again through the proboscis.

A frog which has been eaten in this way by a water-bug can be a surprising sight. It has every appearance of being alive, its eyes are clear and bright, its skin is moist and the position of the body seems normal. But if it is removed from the water it bursts like a balloon, all the inner

Facing page, top two water-striders swimming through the water, with one in the process of eating a spider

Centre two dragonflies mating while in flight

Bottom dragonflies (*Erytroma najas*) laying their eggs on the surface of stagnant water

Below the butterfly *Heteropterus morpheus*, although it does not live exclusively in wetland, comes there to drink

46

juices pour out and the eyes cloud over, leaving only an empty, withered skin.

Another common species of hemiptera which spends its entire life-cycle in the water is the water-boatman (*Notonecta glauca*). It, too, lives on other creatures, especially insects. Its hind legs are covered with bristles and it has a long, tapered body, the optimal shape from the hydrodynamic point of view, which means that it can swim very fast, as fast as the water-beetle in fact. It is in the habit of floating and swimming upside down, for which there is a specific reason: its respiratory organs are situated at the end of the abdomen and therefore, when it surfaces in order to breathe, it requires the abdomen to protrude from the water. Mosquito larvae are a favourite prey of this insect. It will approach its victim, particularly when the latter has, in its turn, surfaced to take in air again through the protruding end of the abdomen. It will then hold it with its front legs, extract the juices through the proboscis and dispose of the empty carcase.

The mosquito itself is a creature always associated with humid regions. It lays its eggs in water, they hatch in water and the larvae live in water. These larvae have a long body with a tube at the end of the abdomen through which they can breathe, suspended just below the water surface. The comma-shaped chrysalis also lives in water. They have many enemies among other water creatures, including water-boatmen, water-beetles and numerous fish, which is fortunate as it serves to limit their numbers.

One fish in particular, the gambusia (*Gambusia affinis*), which comes originally from America but has been imported into Europe and various other parts of the world, is known for the avid way in which it devours the mosquito larvae and chrysales. This tiny fish is only a few centimetres long but has an insatiable appetite. It has become accustomed to European environment and there are no pools or marshes in which it is not at home. It is, perhaps, best known for its ability to adapt to even the most adverse climatic conditions. In Europe it has few problems, but in its native habitat, for instance the Everglades in Florida, it has to face an annual drought which almost completely dries up the marsh. Fortunately, the particular shape of its mouth is such as to enable it to remain alive. Furthermore it has a good, if somewhat unexpected, ally in the alligator in this battle for

Above the guppy has an insatiable appetite and is one of the fish responsible for destroying large numbers of mosquito larvae and pupae

Previous pages a heron on the banks of a pool, photographed shortly after catching an eel

normal level, and a new life-cycle begins.

Returning to the marsh insects, there are some species of Hemiptera which spend their entire lives in the water, even as fully matured adults. These include the ranatra (*Ranatra linearis*), which has a long thin body, and the nepa or water-scorpion (*Nepa rubra*), so named because its body is similar in shape to the scorpion though the abdomen is more squat. At the end of the abdomen is an excrescence containing a slender respiratory tube which enables it to breathe without emerging from the water. Its movements are slow and awkward and it spends all its life among the underwater vegetation, always on the alert and ready to use its strong front legs to capture passing larvae.

Most aquatic insects, however, spend only the early stages of their lives in the water. Among these are some species of trichoptera, such as the caddisfly which is a very strange creature. The larval stage lasts for several months and, though its characteristics vary according to the species, they do follow a fairly set pattern. The larva has an insatiable appetite and a love of comfort and calm, which it provides by constructing a sort of portable case. It has a gland which secretes a type of strong silk, so that all the larva has to do is find suitable material to cement together – gravel, grains of sand, pieces of shell, plant-debris and the like. From these it builds a solid case which is cylindrical or conical in shape and is open at both ends. A larva crawls into each of these cases with its abdomen towards the narrower end and a double hook at the posterior end of the body secures it firmly to the wall. The interior of these tiny houses is lined with a soft silk. If there is any sign of danger the larva slips the fore part of its body out of the shell and drags itself away, with the case trailing behind. It also goes in search of food in this way, piercing the stalks of reeds in order to extract the sap and nibbling at underwater plants and leaves which have fallen on to the surface of the water. But if it should happen to find a mayfly, a tired or injured adult caddisfly or even the body of a dead dragonfly, it has no difficulty in switching from a vegetarian to a carnivorous diet. It will then devour anything it finds down to the last morsel, as it requires an enormous amount of food (around three times it own body-weight) in order to live and grow.

The larva grows rapidly, which means that it is constantly having to enlarge its protective case. The aspect which most typifies the be-

survival. There are two essential characteristics which aquatic animals must develop in order to survive periods of drought: they must be able to combat dehydrations and asphyxiation and to reproduce and propagate quickly as soon as the rainy season returns. The gambusia, which is viviparous – produces its young alive instead of hatching – has managed to adapt very successfully in both these respects.

During the dry season the marsh bed is reduced to a mass of caked mud which becomes extremely hard and cracked. There are only a few isolated holes where there is a little water or wet mud. These are known in the Everglades as 'gator holes', because they are sought out by alligators trying to escape the drought. All the aquatic creatures, in particular the fish, find their way to these holes in an attempt to avoid asphyxiation and dehydration, but only a few actually survive there. These are generally the gambusia and other small fish of the same family with similarly shaped bodies. All other species die within a few days and the pool is reduced to a watery mud in which only the gambusia and related species remain.

The survival of these particular species can almost certainly be attributed to the shape of their mouth. The upper section is completely flat and the mouth inclines upwards towards the top of the head. Thus the fish can swim in the normal position and breathe in water which is in direct contact with the surface and consequently rich in oxygen. Other species are unable to take advantage of this reserve of oxygen and therefore die. When the rains begin again the gambusia is quick to spread throughout the marsh, as soon as the water returns to its

haviour of these insects, however, is the system by which some species obtain their food. It is, in fact, very effective and highly original in that they capture the maximum amount of prey with the minimum effort and risk to themselves. They weave underwater nets from a silk thread which they produce themselves, often reinforced with plant filaments. These nets are then placed in the most favourable positions, i.e. the most likely spots for capturing young fish and other small aquatic creatures. They are usually attached firmly to the stalks of underwater plants and positioned in areas well penetrated by sunlight and popular with small marsh creatures. Often the larva will place the net near those parts of the marsh inhabited by the more dangerous predators. If the victims escape the first hazard they will find themselves entangled in the traps set by the caddisfly, which lies in wait in the corner of the net ready to devour the unfortunate creatures.

Other insects which spend the early stages of their lives in the water include the mayfly, the generic order of which is known as the Ephemeroptera because the imago has a lifespan of only one day, the stonefly (*Perla maxima*) and numerous species of Diptera. Particularly worthy of mention are the flies of the Tabanidae family, the larvae of which live in water or soft mud. Many adult species of horsefly are bloodsuckers and can inflict quite a painful sting on man and animals. These particular Diptera

Below a species of horse-fly, *Ochrops*, these flies have huge, brilliantly coloured eyes

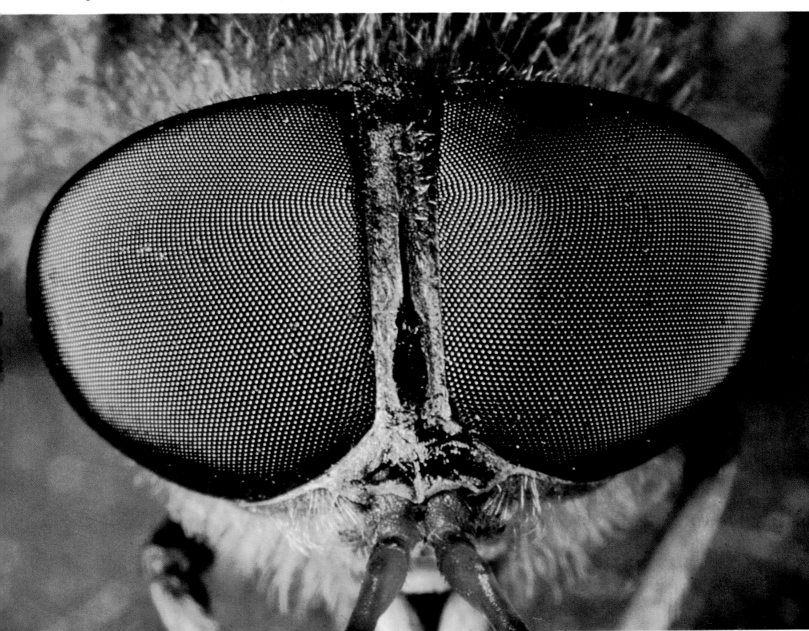

have large eyes composed of thousands of ommatidia, or facets, and in some species the colours and reflections are quite wonderful.

The dragonfly is another typical marsh inhabitant. It is carnivorous throughout all stages of its development. The larvae feed on other insects, worms, tadpoles, young newts and young fish. Generally their colouring is dull and uninteresting and they live submerged in the mud or concealed among the vegetation. They do not go in search of prey nor do they set off in pursuit of it, but lie in wait until it comes within range.

The dragonfly larva has an elongated lower lip, protruding like an additional limb, at the end of which is a hook used to secure the prey. When this lip isn't required it lies folded along the side of the body, but as soon as there is any sign of prey within range it flashes into action, powerful muscles seizing the victim and transfering it to the mouth of the larva. This lower lip can then be used as a sort of tray to collect any crumbs of food which drop as the larva is eating.

Depending on the species, the dragonfly remains in the larval stage for anything from a few months to several years. During this time it will undergo a certain number of moults, up to a maximum of fifteen, when the insect will change the skin it has outgrown. When it reaches the final stage the larva affixes itself firmly to the stalk of a plant, then after a series of complicated contortions the adult emerges from the skin. It is still soft and colourless and has to wait until its skin and in particular its wings are completely dry before it can begin to fly.

The dragonfly imago is a ferocious predator. The back of its head, which seems to be attached to its body by a single thread, is concave in shape, allowing the insect to turn its compound eyes in all directions in search of prey. Some species of dragonfly have eyes so large that they touch in the centre of the head. Their thousands of ommatidia, situated at every possible angle, give the insect all-round , panoramic vision. It has two powerful jaws lined with tiny teeth, from which the order of insects to which the dragonfly belongs derive the name Odonata. It uses these teeth to devour the insects on which it feeds – mosquitoes, small flies, tiny Hemiptera and sometimes also larger insects, including other dragonflies. While it is in flight, its long, thin legs are folded to form a sort of basket in which it catches its prey. Its wings are very long, strong and flexible and it is extremely skilled in the air. The older species of winged insect have developed a sophisticated method of flight which they have used for millions of years and which perhaps goes some way towards explaining their amazing ability to withstand the geological changes that have taken place around them.

The four wings each have individual muscles, which means that the front and rear sets can move independently of one another, allowing the insect a wide range of manoeuvre. The dragonfly can remain in the air for some time, dancing and swooping, and it is also able to hover motionless for a few moments like a miniature helicopter. A speed of approximately 90 km per hour has been recorded for some species in full flight. They are so adapted to life in the air that some will mate in flight and others lay their eggs while skimming over the surface of the water. Often in mid or late summer the female can be seen flying low over the surface of the water. Every so often she will drop down, just grazing the surface, and then rise again to her original position. She will do this repeatedly, depositing an egg on the surface each time she touches it. Other species will take up a position on the water with the abdomen completely immersed in order to lay their eggs on a twig or underwater plant.

Not all dragonflies display skill in the air. Those belonging to the suborder known as Zygoptera, which includes the graceful damselfly, are slow and awkward and an easy catch for insectivorous birds. These dragonflies, which are again carnivorous, have fairly singular habits. During copulation the male uses the pincers at the tip of his abdomen to clasp the female behind her head, with the two bodies forming a sort of heart shape. Immediately after mating the female lays her eggs, plunging the end of her abdomen into the water and depositing them on the surface of submerged leaves. For a short while the male remains attached to her, holding her behind the head, and then flies off with his body practically vertical.

There are some species of insect which prefer to live on the surface of the water. These are strong swimmers, such as the Coleoptera of the Gyrinidae family which circle in large groups on the surface. At the slightest hint of danger they will dive under the water. The Gyrinidae, equally at home in air and water, are strong enough to fly to a new pool or marsh if the one in which they have made their home shows signs

Below, left the ladybird is one of many insects who feed on aphids

Below, right ants of the species *Crematogaster scutellaris*; they are so fond of the sugary liquid secreted by the aphid that they even carry them away when danger threatens

of drying up. They can collect a bubble of air on their abdomen and this enables them to remain immersed in the water. Their eyes are divided into an upper and lower section, which means the insect is able to see both the air above it and the water below.

Another surface insect, a species of Hemiptera, is the water-strider of the genus *Gerris*. They have a long, thin body with short forelegs and very long centre and hind legs. They hold their forelegs out of the water and use them to capture small insects, spiders and other creatures which have fallen on the water. The centre legs

act as oars and the hind ones as rudders. They are not just able to glide along with ease on the surface of the water but can also jump and dive without getting wet, because their body is protected by a coat of fine velvety hair and the air trapped in it throws them back out of the water and keeps them completely dry. They glide along the surface without disturbing it by using their legs in a particular way. The claws are not right at the end, as is normally the case, but positioned slightly higher up. At the end of the leg is a tuft of hair which acts like a snow-shoe, enabling the insect to walk on the surface of the

water without breaking it. The water-strider performs all its main functions, from feeding to mating, while gliding over the water in this way.

An even more numerous group is that of the insects which live in the air above the marsh. They include all types of creature, flying, crawling, climbing, etc., vegetarian insects which live on the luscious marsh vegetation, and predator insects which feed on other insect species and thus preserve a balance in the environment. Some of these pass the early stages of their lives in the water, while others spend their

Below a female aphid giving birth by parthenogenesis

entire lives in the air. These creatures, too, form part of fairly complex food-chains. For example, aphids living on the sap of plants are in their turn food for other insect species such as ladybirds, lacewing larvae and some species of Diptera, particularly those of the hover-fly family (Syrphidae). The latter, despite being the keenest in the air, are often preyed upon by insectivorous birds and even dragonflies. The dragonfly may in turn be the victim of birds or frogs and the frog may then fall prey to a heron, water-rail, grebe or even a water-snake. The last of these is eaten by many birds of prey. In fact there are so many possible combinations of predator and prey in the marsh environment that it would take hundreds of pages to develop them all fully.

In periods of drought the marsh and wet areas in general attract numerous species not native to these regions which come there in search of water and coolness. Bees, wasps, hornets and numerous brightly coloured butterfly species will alight on clumps of seaweed or plants saturated with water or on the wet mud in order to suck in the water they require. Innumerable varieties of butterfly can be seen among the reeds, rushes and cat's-tails. Some species of nymphalid, like the *Nymphalis io* and *N. atalanta*, are found at the edges of the marsh where the reeds are interspersed with clumps of nettles on which the larvae feed. Others, such as the Camberwell Beauty (*N. antiopa*), prefer the shrubs and trees of the undergrowth surrounding the marsh.

Still other butterflies, such as the European Swallowtail (*Papilio machaon*), will fly swiftly over the tops of the reeds and settle for an instant on a flower in order to suck up the nectar. They are sometimes found inland but prefer shady coastal marshes. Just the opposite preference is exhibited by a butterfly from southern Europe, the *Heodes dispar-continentalis*, in that it lives in inland marshes. Although small, it is considered to be one of the most beautiful species found in this region. In May it will often be seen to flit from one cat's-tail to another in a courtship dance.

There are some marsh insects so small and unobtrusive that their presence goes almost unnoticed. When they are chanced upon, in among the most dense clumps of reeds and cat's-tails, this can provide an unpleasant surprise as hands and clothing become stained with a greenish-brown liquid deposited on the

Above the *Ceresa bubalus*, a species of homoptera which can in the early stages of its life camouflage itself effectively among the vegetation

plants by hordes of aphids.

Their particular method of reproduction accounts for the incredible numbers of aphids. Members of both sexes are born towards the end of summer. They mate and the females lay eggs which are hardy enough to withstand the rigours of winter. In spring the females which hatch from these eggs reproduce by parthenogenesis. Up to sixteen generations may be produced in this way in a year. This both simplifies and accelerates the life-cycle. Numbers would increase thus ad infinitum if it were not for the fact that the aphid has many enemies, including both the larva and imago of the ladybird (*Coccinella*). Ohter insects which prey on it are the lacewing (*Chrysopa*) and related species. Lacewing larvae, incidentally, clothe themselves in the empty shells of aphids they have

devoured.

Certain Diptera species of the Syrphidae family play an important part in the control of aphids. These are known as hover-flies because they are able to come to an abrupt halt in flight by beating their wings furiously and producing a sort of gyroscopic effect. They can then set off again in any direction – backwards, forwards, sideways, upwards or downwards – come to a stop for an instant and then set off again without alighting anywhere. The larvae of these insects will creep up on a colony of aphids which remain stock-still, as if paralysed, until the predator has feasted.

The aphids do, however, have friends as well as enemies. These are species of ant which are so fond of the sugary liquid secreted by the aphids that they will care most attentively for them,

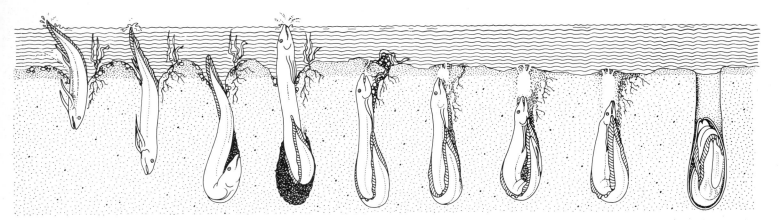

Above how the mudfish survives the dry season by burying itself in the mud

to the extent of either removing them from any danger which might threaten or making some attempt to defend them.

Some species of mantid may also be found in the leaves of marsh vegetation, among them the praying mantis (*Mantis religiosa*), a ferocious predator always on the alert and ready to capture some unlucky insect. The marsh environment is also the home of numerous Coleoptera and Hemiptera. Some species of the latter type worthy of mention are the delicately hued Homoptera, such as the *Erotettix cyanae*; a small bluish Hemiptera which lives among water-lilies and pond weed; and the North American buffalo treehopper (*Ceresa bubalus*), a strange triangular Hemiptera which is at home in a wet environment or on a river bank.

The marsh fauna also includes many vertebrates. One fish which merits a mention is the pike (*Esox lucius*) which preys fiercely on other fish, amphibians, particularly frogs, and some-

times even young water-birds. They prefer areas where the aquatic vegetation is dense and they can lie in wait for their prey. The marsh may also be the home of tench (*Tinca tinca*) which swim along the mud bed feeding on small animals. Carp also favour the muddy waters. Their suspicious nature and slowness allows them to live to a fairly advanced age and they grow up to a metre in length.

In some places, such as the Comacchio valley, Italy, one of the main species of fish is the eel. They are born in the depths of the ocean and spend the first year of their lives there. Then, as if obeying some primeval instinct, they make their way through the same waters negotiated by generations before them in order to reproduce. How they cover considerable distance overland to reach small pools and remote marshes is well known.

The marsh is also an ideal habitat for numerous amphibians, which spend the early stages of their lives in water and still require it once they reach adulthood, both to keep their skin moist and for the purposes of reproduction. Of all the amphibians living in European marshes and wetlands the most numerous species is undoubtedly the edible frog (*Rana esculenta*). During the summer the croaking of the males echoes all round the marsh. Unlike other species they are not content just to cry at night, and when the sky is overcast or stormy their monotonous call can be heard everywhere. The noise is produced partly from sacs situated below the throat and partly from the mouth. These are filled with air and act as resonance chambers. The male will emit this sound as a mating cry and leap through the reeds and marsh grasses, dive into the water, reappear and dive again without pausing, all in search of a mate. When he eventually finds one he will hold her in front of him, mounting on her back and grasping her

Below the waterboatman is an adept swimmer; it prefers to live in still or slowmoving waters

Left, top the yellow-bellied toad is one of the most attractively coloured members of the toad family found in western Europe

Centre a typical pond frog caught in mid 'song'

Bottom the strange position adopted by the green frog, with part of its head submerged

with the suckers on the toes of his hind legs. Other batrachians, such as the common toad (*Bufo bufo*), and the yellow-bellied toad (*Bombina variegata*) also copulate in this way. The latter is perhaps the most beautiful of all the species to be found in western Europe. Although it is rather squat and its back is brownish in colour, its belly is a splendid yellow or orange with blue spots. A related species, the fire-bellied toad (*Bombina bombina*), has an even more striking red-and-blue colouring but is found only in eastern Europe.

The spawn of the frog is laid in clusters, completely encased in a jelly-like substance and attached to the bed vegetation. Within a

couple of weeks tadpoles hatch from it. These can often grow to be longer than the adult frog, which is rarely more than about 10 cm.

Tadpoles are often victims of predators such as carnivorous insect larvae and birds but sufficient numbers survive to keep the species on the increase. Insects and worms are the favourite food of adult frogs. They are, however, unable to eat under water or to swallow the young fish which swim near the banks and would make an easy catch. The amiable little tree-toad (*Hyla arborea*), one of the tiniest frogs found in European marshes, lives in the water only while laying its eggs. At other times it prefers to remain in the open among the reeds, foliage and other undergrowth. In fine weather they will be seen to lie motionless on the tops of leaves but they are ready to move to the underside of the leaf if the sun proves too strong or if it begins to rain. Their incessant, strident cry can be heard some distance away, especially in springtime. But they will also emit their cry in summer during wet weather or after a storm. Unlike the common frog their voice-box is located under the throat and when filled with air it can expand to twice the size of the creature's head.

Other amphibians found in the marsh environment are generally calmer and less noisy than the frog. These include the common newt (*Triturus cristatus*), which is dark-brown with slight greyish tinges and consequently not easily seen. During the mating season the males take on a much more colourful appearance: a combed crest forms on their back extending from the nape of the neck to the tip of the tail.

Below a newt at the end of the larval stage. Dark in colour, it will take on a brighter appearance during the mating season

Bottom larval stage of the Alpine newt, a species found only in mountain marshes and lakes

Being transparent, it reflects the sun's rays and is quite beautiful to look at.

The male makes great play during the initial stages of courtship, swimming round and round his mate and following after her for some time. Then at a particular point he bars her way and brings himself closer until their heads touch. Usually he keeps his legs rigid and his back arched. Then he turns his tail towards the female and strikes her on the sides. Finally he sinks down flat with his body contracted and releases a spermatophore. The female brings herself up towards him and the spermatophore is thus introduced into her genital organs. This process may be repeated numerous times, until the male eventually swims off in search of a new mate. Small, yellowish-green larvae hatch from the eggs. These carnivorous larvae are characterised by a virtual crown of branched gills round their heads.

The favourite foods of the newt are molluscs, worms and the larvae of various species and they thus contribute to maintaining a balance among the numerous small marsh creatures. Other species of newt fairly common in marsh environments are the *Triturus vulgaris* and *T. alpestris*, though the latter is found only in alpine pools and marshes.

Typical marsh predators are the reptiles. These include the European pond tortoise (*Emys orbicularis*), which is so timid that it is difficult to study its behaviour at all. It is artful and always quick to bury its dark shell in among the muddy waters near the banks, leaving only its head visible. It will dive for tadpoles, newts and fish, devouring them under the water, and it will sometimes attack snakes or even steal eggs and nestlings from nests on the surface.

The behaviour of snakes, such as the grass-snake (*Natrix natrix*) and water-serpents (*N. maura* and *N. tassellata*) are numerous and easy to spot as they weave their way across the surface of the water, always ready to dive and hide on the bottom at the least sign of danger. They feed mainly on frogs, tadpoles and fish, but they are also very fond of eggs and when they find colonies of terns or gulls they are quite capable of eating chicks from the nest. The particular anatomy of their mouths allows them to swallow mouthfuls larger than themselves. They are able to open their mouths as wide as this because there is no join between the two sides of their jaws.

With certain qualifications, birds can generally be said to occupy an even higher position in the food-chain than reptiles. An exception here is the tortoise which, protected by its shell, has practically no enemies. On the other hand snakes will be preyed upon by rapacious birds and perhaps even a hungry heron, but will in their turn feed on the eggs or young of these same birds. It is, nevertheless, justifiable to place them in a higher position because, all in all, they are more often the predator than the victim.

More will be said about the birds, the virtual lords of the marsh, in the next chapter. For the moment we will confine ourselves to considering their position in the marsh ecosystem. Many bird species feed on creatures of lower orders such as frogs and fish. This creates a complex series of aggressive and competitive relationships between predators and prey and also between various predator species and individuals within particular species. Nature has,

however, managed to arrange things in such a way that each individual and each species occupies a well-defined position within the whole system.

Each bird species has its own position in the hierarchy. Disputes and conflicts may bring about changes in the order, resulting in a classification fought out by the birds themselves. Thus each individual is in a superior position to some species but is inferior to others, though there must, of course, be one species at the top.

If one member of the bird community should find itself unable to ward off attacks from another bird lower down the scale it loses its position. The bird which moves up to the higher position vacates a space over which birds in the lower orders, including the one who has been displaced, will then fight. It is possible to observe this pattern of behaviour in birds when they are in search of food. An apparently disorderly group will soon establish

Below the pond tortoise is the only member of the turtle family found in inland waters in Europe. It feeds on small creatures which it captures, generally at night

themselves into a social hierarchy within a species and a generic structure among the different species which inhabit the same territory.

The marsh will often be the home of several species of heron, such as the night heron (*Nycticorax nycticorax*), the egret (*Egretta garzetta*), the purple heron (*Ardea purpurea*) and the blue-grey heron (*A. cinerea*). They all feed mainly on fish and frogs but have developed different methods of capturing their prey. They very rarely come into conflict as each species has its own hunting ground. The small night heron remains in the shallow waters near the banks, while the larger blue-grey heron prefers to search for food in deeper waters and the various other species select a depth which suits the length of their legs. The similar anatomy of all the species, combined with their different methods of capturing their prey and their preferences for different areas of the marsh, are all factors which contribute to reducing competition between them. The territory at their disposal and food resources are divided among the various species to the benefit of them all, in that they make the fullest use of their environment. If they were all to hunt for their food in the same place they would inevitably fight over it, to the detriment of the different species as a whole and of specific individuals.

Examples of insects which have a distinct larval stage associated with marshes and still-running water.

INSECT	LARVAL TYPE	ADULT TYPE
Mayfly Order Ephemeroptera	Aquatic nymphs are nocturnal. Distinguished by three long tail appendages. Plant-feeders.	Short-lived (1 day to 1 week). Fly above the water e.g. *Cloeon*.
Dragonfly Order Odonoata	Aquatic larva carnivorous – with a 'mask' having strong claws. Lives 1 to 2 years.	Fast-flying predators e.g. *Aeshna*.
Stone-fly Order Plecoptera	Aquatic larva has a flattened body. Mainly vegetarian. Lives 1 to 3 years.	There are few still-water species e.g. *Perla*. Adults live 2 to 3 weeks.
Alder-fly Order Neuroptera	Aquatic larva is carnivorous. Lives up to 2 years.	Free-flying e.g. *Sialis*.
Caddis-fly Order Trichoptera	Most larva living in still water protect themselves by making tubes of stone, sand, twigs etc.	Fly at dusk. Look like small moths but have hairy wings e.g. *Anabolia*.
Crane-fly Order Diptera	Aquatic larva is worm-like with extensions on last body segment.	Typical 'daddy-long-legs' e.g. *Tipula*.
Drone-fly Order Diptera	The larva known as the rat-tailed maggot has a long fine breathing tube.	Drone-fly *Eristalis*.
Gnat Order Diptera	Larva and pupa aquatic.	Male gnats can be seen swarming near water in early autumn e.g. *Culex*.
Water beetle Order Coleoptera	Larva 'stands' in an upright position. Extremely voracious. Sucks out the body of its prey.	Members of the genus *Dytiscus* are aquatic and feed on prey much larger than themselves.

63

Chapter Three
The Lords of the Marsh

*It has been estimated that of the 476 bird species
to be found in Europe as many as 188 species are associated with a marsh
or lagoon environment. This chapter describes the appearance
and habits of many birds which depend on access to a marshland environment
and goes on to show how the loss of these areas could have a drastic effect
on migration routes and nesting habits.*

Facing page
The purple heron nests in colonies, generally among the
reeds and only occasionally in bushes or trees

Of those birds who can be said to assume a proprietary interest in the marsh environment the most impressive *en masse* are the mallards. Suddenly they will rise in a great cloud, their multi-hued wings like a firework exploding in the sky, as if to establish their superiority. In fact there are numerous birds which have made their homes in marshland throughout the world, in particular in the temperate zones. These are migratory birds which use the marsh as an intermediate stop on their long flights, birds which remain there throughout the year and still others which come there during the mating season, remaining until their offspring have grown.

Numerous winged species, therefore, gravitate for one reason or another towards marsh or wetlands. It has been estimated that of the 476 European bird species as many as 188 are associated in some way with the marsh or lagoon environment. Despite the number of eggs they lay and their ability to recover in the face of adversity, the future of these aquatic birds is threatened by a number of factors. Other species have thousands of square miles available to them but the marsh birds are restricted to areas where there is water. For example migratory species, that is those which nest in the northern or north-eastern tundra of Europe and spend the winter in southern Italy or Africa, find the lagoons and marshes invaluable for recuperation and as sources for food.

The loss of these environments through drainage or pollution could have a drastic effect on those migration routes: even greater would be the loss to those species which actually nest in the marsh, such as the coot (*Fulica atra*), the mallard (*Anas platyrhynca*), the black-winged stilt (*Himantopus himantopus*) and many others. They are also menaced by the number of people who indulge in shooting as a sport, often destroying an unacceptably high proportion of the bird and animal kingdom.

Facing page, top a purple heron in full flight. To avoid conflict with each other, the various species of marsh heron keep to their own hunting grounds

Bottom the blue-grey heron is often sighted in southern Europe. If the climatic conditions are favourable it will remain throughout the year in the same spot

Below an egret skims over the waters of a stagnant pool

In other parts of the world the situation is not much better. According to reliable estimates, the number of duck in North America was originally between 250 and 500 million. In 1824, when trapper Jim Bridger first navigated the Bear River by canoe as far as Great Salt Lake, he found the sky completely filled by an immense cloud of duck and his path was closely followed by the professional hunters who had already wreaked havoc on the duck population of the eastern parts of the country. In 1887 one hunter shot nearly two thousand birds in just one season and another took 335 in a day. Hunting has continued through the years, diminishing the number of duck to such an extent that there have recently been fears for the existence of the species. In addition to shooting, the majority of available wetlands, marshes, pools, etc., have been lost through drainage, and numerous nesting areas in the Canadian prairies are also likely to be drained in time, striking at the heart of the duck's existence. In recent years the United States has tried to remedy the situation by establishing a network of more than two hundred sanctuaries for water-birds, over a total of more than three million acres.

The appearance, elegance, behaviour patterns and, in some cases, colouring of the different marsh birds all combine to make a very varied and attractive community. Some species feed on plants, while others are predators. Some are solitary creatures, others tend to band together in large groups, particularly in the nesting season. In some cases the birds in these colonies are all of the same species; for example a heronry may comprise several heron species. The aim of the birds in banding together in this way is probably one of defence against predators.

The herons as a whole are perhaps the most typical birds of the marsh in that they are associated throughout their lives with an aquatic environment. The best known of the European herons is probably the blue-grey heron (*Ardea cinerea*), an extremely elegant bird which can measure up to a metre from the tip of its beak to the end of its tail and has a wing-span of approximately 1.80 m. It has long, thin legs, a graceful and very mobile neck and a long, firm beak. Both the male and female have the same colouring, though the plumage of the young is greyer than that of the adult birds.

These herons will spend the night high in the trees which surround the marsh, safe from attack. When dawn breaks they will come down on to the banks and advance slowly and carefully into the water to begin their day's fishing, which can last for several hours at a time. They will feed on fish, eels, frogs and even water-snakes. If the climatic conditions are favourable, the herons will live all the year round in the same place. But if the winter temperatures fall too low they prefer to migrate, sometimes to a considerable distance away.

During the mating season they normally band together in fairly sizeable colonies, associating freely with other species of heron, such as the squacco, the egret or the night heron. Pairs will carry out the necessary repairs and re-use the previous year's nests, or, if need be, will build new nests from reeds, straw and twigs heaped together preferably in tree forks. One tree can contain many nests of this type.

Another species similar to the blue-grey heron is the purple heron (*Ardea purpurea*). It is smaller and darker in colour with a reddish-brown plumage. Unlike the blue-grey variety it prefers to nest among the reeds, often together with other heron species. These heronries are a marvellous sight, consisting in some cases of several hundreds or even thousands of birds from different species. Should the inhabitants feel threatened by an intruder, they will rise almost simultaneously in flight, emitting an alarm cry and circling low over the marsh until they are sure it is safe to return. Various species are found in these heronries, including herons, night herons, squaccos and egrets. The eggs and young are all so alike that the only way to discover with certainty which nest belongs to which species is to remain concealed until the parents return to their young, believing the danger to be over.

The purple heron's nest consists of a platform of reeds designed simply for soundness and camouflaged among the reeds. This heron is a particularly careful and circumspect bird, as if trying by its cautious movements and arched neck to imitate a snake. Once an egg has been

Right two squacco herons on their nest built in the thick of the reeds. Also clearly visible are two newly hatched chicks

Far right, top the little bittern is a solitary bird which lives among dense vegetation on river banks, round stagnant pools or in marshy woodlands

Bottom little bittern with young nestlings

laid it will go through the most elaborate precautions before approaching the nest. Usually the parents take it in turns to tend the nest, while the other goes in search of food.

The hand-over of guard duty from one parent to another is a sight not to be missed; the heron which has been absent circles overhead to check that it is safe to land. Even if he sees no sign of danger he will not attempt to approach the nest until his mate gives him the all-clear from below, in the form of a short, raucous cry. Only when he has received this signal will he decide to land. He never makes directly for the nest but touches down nearby, or, if danger threatens, some distance away in the thick of the reeds. From there he begins to approach, his long legs stepping carefully from one clump of reeds to the next.

Even the watcher in the hide awaiting his arrival is taken by surprise when he appears suddenly from among the reeds. But the heron is not quite at his destination. He still has to get astride the nest without dislodging it and upsetting the eggs into the water. Like a tightrope walker he carefully positions first one foot and then the other and finally lowers himself on to the nest. In the meantime his mate is preparing in turn to fly away. This departure is often preceded by a fairly complex ritual consisting of an exchange of cries and a series of movements in which the bird will extend its wings, ruffle its body feathers and raise those on its head like a comb. Some species of heron complete this ceremony in a curious way in that the bird coming to take over guard will bear a twig in its beak. Most pairs of herons work jointly on construction of the nest; once it is finished the bringing of a twig at each hand-over has a purely symbolic significance.

The eggs will take several weeks to hatch but the young do not all appear at the same time. This can sometimes have unfortunate consequences as the first born, being bigger and stronger, will often occupy the parents' full attention and most of the food will find its way into their mouths, leaving those which hatched late to go hungry. Often the parents do not realise what is happening because they are so busy searching for food that, after the first few days, they no longer feed the chicks individually

Above the night heron, which lives in dense vegetation on waterlogged land

Below each heron species has a different method of fishing: the white heron **A** and green heron **F** stand in wait for their prey; the little blue heron **B** catches passing fish; the red egret **C** and the Louisiana heron **D** spread their wings to create a shadow and thus attract fish; and the white egret **E** terrifies its prey by beating the water with its legs

but lay the food on the edge of the nest and allow the young to distribute it among themselves. It is, therefore, quite easy for the stronger nestlings to deprive the weaker ones of food, with the result that they can die of starvation in the nest without the parents showing much sign of concern, except at best to dispose of them by pushing the bodies out into the water.

Some time after the eggs have hatched the nest will become coated in a thick layer of excrement, corresponding with the nestlings' equally rapid growth. Within a few months these ugly chicks with their untidy, downy feathers acquire a sleek new coat and strong wings and at last begin to become recognisable as herons. During this same period, the parents teach them how to use their beaks to catch fish and frogs. After a few days they are made to fend for themselves and shortly afterwards all the birds leave the heronry, to return *en masse* the following year.

One heron species which has become comparatively rare in southern Europe is the white heron (*Casmerodius albus*). But there are two other species which are similar, though considerably smaller, such as the egret (*Egretta garzetta*) and squacco (*Ardeola ralloides*). The first of these nests in trees, while the latter prefers thick reed beds. It resembles the purple heron in this respect and also in the way in which it builds its nest, the caution of its approach and the manner in which it tends its young.

One of the smallest members of the heron family is the little bittern (*Ixobrychus minutus*), which has somewhat singular habits. It will generally shun all forms of social contact, living a solitary existence and accompanying its mate only during the mating season and while the eggs are hatching. Of reddish-grey plumage with black streaks, its movements are slow and cautious and it will launch itself in flight by beating its wings awkwardly. During the day it will fly just above the tops of the reeds but at night it will soar high in the sky, often emitting a strident cry. When coming in to land it glides low over the undergrowth, then folds its

Previous page, top ruffs in flight over the Po delta

Bottom The grace and elegance of a group of flamingoes flying over the Rhône delta

Below the snipe uses its long, thin bill to search the mud for worms and other small creatures

wings and drops straight down into the reeds. One particular characteristic is its ability to camouflage itself among the vegetation, especially when it is on the nest and senses danger: it will crouch up on its legs, extend its neck, head and beak, draw its squat, clumsy body into amazingly vertical lines and remain motionless, trying to appear as tall and straight as possible in order to blend in with the reeds and other marsh vegetation. It can disguise itself in this way with remarkable success.

Once the eggs have hatched and the chicks find themselves left alone for a time they, too, are able to conceal themselves cunningly from any would-be attacker. Whenever they hear a strange sound they do not remain waiting in dread but leave their nests and scatter among the surrounding vegetation. In a group they would represent easy prey, but dispersed among the reeds there is every chance they will not be seen. There is no need for them to be able to fly; it is sufficient if they can run for cover.

Sometimes towards the end of spring a strange cry can be heard coming from the heart of the marsh, like the sound of a distant horn. It is the song of the bittern (*Botaurus stellaris*). It can be heard towards the end of the day up to a distance of several miles and is quite unlike the cry of any other bird. There is something uncanny about it. It seems to come from all directions, but it is fairly safe to assume that it emanates from the middle of the reeds where the bittern has made its nest. This nest is not, however, easy to find because, like the little bittern, this bird is an expert in camouflage. If disturbed by a suspicious sound it, too, will extend its neck and head, point its bill skywards and remain perfectly still. Its presence is well concealed as the colour of its feathers merges with the background and its extended neck and beak are easily mistaken for a reed. If it is taken by surprise it will lash out furiously with its strong, sharp beak, as a last and fairly effective form of defence, capable of inflicting quite painful wounds.

One member of the heron family which is

Below the black-winged stilt nests in colonies always near lagoons, building on a clump of reeds or on a mud bank

relatively common in the south of Europe is the night heron (*Nycticorax nycticorax*). Its melancholy cry, somewhat like that of the crow, can often be heard in the neighbourhood of a marsh. As its name suggests it is a nocturnal bird, and lives in wet regions where there is a dense vegetation. During the day it will almost always remain, resting but watchful, either hidden among the vegetation or perched in the treetops, but it will spend the night roaming the marsh, from time to time emitting its mournful cry. It feeds on amphibians, fish and reptiles, especially small water-snakes, and also on insects and crustaceans. It moves quickly and furtively but the slightest suspicious sound will bring it to a standstill. If it is on the branch of a tree it will not only remain motionless but will press itself against the branch believing that it cannot be seen.

In spring the night herons band together in large groups to build their nests either in trees or deep among the reeds. As is the case with many species of heron, the male is faced with the problem of choosing a mate from among a crowd of apparently identical birds. For this reason they have, like other species, developed a courtship ceremony designed to distinguish the two sexes. The male performs a song-and-dance routine around the nest, extending his neck as he moves. Then he spreads his feathers, drops his head almost to his feet and emits a series of specific notes. This curious spectacle seems to hold an irresistible attraction for the females, who are initially held at a distance by the male. Eventually the one he has selected as his mate is allowed to enter the nest, provided her legs indicate by their deep wine-red colour that she is ready to mate. This ritual is as old as the species itself. If any one of the actions isn't performed mating does not take place.

The bird species found in marshes in southern and south-eastern Europe are too numerous to discuss individually. Some live there only during certain seasons and others are seen but rarely, either because the drainage of the marsh-lands has caused them to abandon the migration routes which passed over this region or because their numbers have been greatly diminished by shooting. This is the case with the stork (*Ciconia ciconia*), which now prefers to follow routes over the Iberian or Balkan peninsulas when it migrates northwards. The same is true of the spoonbill (*Platalea leucorodia*), found in southern Spain along the Dutch coast and in the Balkans. The glossy ibis (*Plegadis falcinellus*) can still be seen in the Po valley and occasionally along the coast of Tuscany. The flamingo (*Phoenicepterus ruber*) is still found in fairly large colonies in Sardinia and has been sighted once or twice on the Italian mainland round the Orbetello lagoon in Tuscany, but its main European strongholds are the Marismas del Guadalquivir in Spain and the Camargue in the south of France, where it nests quite regularly.

The pelican (*Pelecanus onocrotalus*) and the Dalmatian pelican (*Pelecanus crispus*) are still found in the Balkans, both in the coastal regions of the southern Adriatic and around the Black Sea, particularly in the Danube delta. They have also been seen occasionally in Italy on the southern Adriatic coast. A much more common species in southern Europe, however, is the black-feathered cormorant (*Phalacrocorax carbo*) which is found in fairly large colonies, for example on Lake Burano in the extreme south of Tuscany. The cattle egret (*Bubulcus ibis*) is a small African heron which is notable for the way it will follow a herd of animals. It is seen from time to time in various parts of Europe and has become firmly established in southern Spain and Portugal. As well as extending its territory in this way, some members of this enterprising species have even managed to find their way to America during the last century and it is now found throughout that continent, from Latin America to Canada. In addition to these species, there are numerous smaller birds inextricably connected with the marsh environment. These are the group known as the waders because they stand on their long legs in muddy water searching for food, generally consisting of crustaceans, molluscs, worms etc.

An interesting bird that nests in northern and central Europe and Scandinavia is the ruff (*Philomachus pugnax*). 'Pugnax' means fighting and thus leaves no doubt as to its nature. It has an elaborate courtship display: the male changes completely in appearance, losing the feathers on the sides and front of its head and replacing them with numerous small but brightly coloured caruncles. Tufts appear on the sides of its head, looking from a distance like peculiar ears, a large ruff of feathers grows on its throat, neck and upper thorax while the remainder of its plumage also changes colour, becoming more of a reddish-brown with large black patches.

Facing page a series of photographs showing the courtship ceremony and mating of a pair of black-winged stilt

Facing page, top
Parent and juvenile
great-crested grebe
Bottom the grebe's
nest floating among
the reeds

Below an avocet
sitting on eggs.
They generally nest
near estuaries or
sand banks, building
near the water
among bushes or
grass

Attired thus in battle livery and with their feathers fluffed out, the males attack one another with their beaks, jumping, feinting and pursuing one another so ferociously that disaster seems inevitable. But, like most animals who open the mating season by fighting, the ruff is not given to cruelty. After a fairly lengthy skirmish one of the contenders will withdraw, little the worse for the battle, and leave the females to the victor, as the ruff is, in fact, polygamous.

Another strange wader bird is the snipe (*Gallinago gallinago*). Here interest lies not so much in its behaviour but more in its appearance, in particular in its disproportionately long, thin beak, which it finds invaluable for hunting. Snipe are usually found singly or in small groups and only rarely in large bands in marshes,

muddy fields and coastal regions. They are most active at dawn and dusk and feed mainly on molluscs, worms and other creatures which they find in the mud or wet, sandy soil. They use their bill like a probe, plunging it methodically into the wet mud, and every so often find a tiny creature which they will quickly devour. The great snipe (*Gallinago media*) is similar to the snipe itself but its bill and legs are shorter.

Other members of this large group of wading birds are the black-tailed godwit (*Limosa limosa*), the bar-tailed godwit (*L. lapponica*), the redshank (*Tringa totanus*), the spotted redshank (*T. erythropus*), the greater yellowlegs (*T. melanoleuca*), the lesser yellowlegs (*T. flavipes*) and the greenshank (*T. nebularia*). One of the larger birds in this group is the curlew (*Numenius arquata*) which can measure more than 50 cm

in length and have a wing-span of up to a metre. Like other members of the sandpiper family, it is a migratory bird, preferring to spend the summer in the fresh northern marshes and the winter in the warmer Mediterranean regions. Some waders, such as the oystercatcher (*Haematopus ostralegus*), the pratincole (*Glareola pratincola*) and the ringed plover (*Charadrius hiaticula*), prefer coastal environments and in particular lagoons and brackish marshes. The little ringed plover (*C. dubius*) will spend the winter on the sea coast but moves inland during the other seasons. It prefers to nest on the pebbly or sandy shores of rivers, laying its eggs among the stones. The eggs are so well camouflaged they confuse predators into mistaking them for stones. The Kentish plover (*C. alexandrinus*) has similar nesting habits to the little ringed species.

Another small but elegant wader found in marshy environments is the lapwing (*Vanellus vanellus*), distinguishable by its small crested head. In spring the top feathers of the male become a sleek brown with bronze and purple streaks and its wings are black with blue tinges. In the morning and evening it will fly over pools and marshes in search of food. If it senses danger it will raise the alarm by emitting a long strident, whistling cry. This explains why the lapwing, which is also fairly common in central and southern Asia, is known there as the 'sentinel of the rice fields'.

There are two further birds in this group outstanding for the beauty of their form – the black-winged stilt and the avocet. The black-winged stilt (*Himantopus himantopus*) has remarkably long and slender legs in proportion to the size of its body. They are a dazzling coral-pink and, when the stilt steps into the water in search of food, it does so with the precision of a ballerina. Sightings of this bird seem to depend on the climatic conditions. Today it's to be seen mostly in Spain and central and southern Asia, but toward the middle of the last century it was found frequently in Italy and used to nest in Tuscany and Sicily. The climate then was appreciably cooler and the frequency with which this elegant marsh bird was seen certainly decreased during the warm spell which began in 1885 and lasted for approximately the next fifty years. The present cycle would seem to be one of low temperatures and, as might be anticipated, the black-winged stilt has again begun to nest in Italy.

The black-winged stilt will guard its territory jealously. If, during the nesting season, any intruder tries to approach the nest, one, or sometimes both, parents will immediately rise in the air and circle over the head of the unwelcome guest, emitting raucous cries until the latter is forced to leave. If this fails, or if a more serious danger threatens, the bird will resort to further defence tactics. For example, if a predator approaches dangerously near to its nest it will pretend to be injured and in difficulty, flying erratically with its legs hanging and wings partly contracted. The performance is so realistic that the predator is deceived and tries to approach what appears to be a sure catch. As it draws closer the stilt always manages to edge a little further away, taking the predator with it. Once it judges the predator to be a safe distance from the nest, it will suddenly 'recover' and fly off, leaving the creature dumbfounded.

The skill which the black-winged stilt displays in defending its territory is equally evident when it comes to finding migration routes through the skies. This has recently been demonstrated quite remarkably: a squadron of helicopters from the Swedish Air Force followed a flock of black-winged stilt over the open sea as far as Scotland. The observation which emerged from this is clearly that while the helicopters were obliged to use complicated calculations in order to stay on course, the birds were able to correct the direction of their flight automatically, as if guided by some invisible radar system. The way in which birds use the sun and stars to navigate their journeys makes a fascinating study.

No less beautiful and elegant than the black-winged stilt is the avocet (*Recurvirostra avosetta*). Its most characteristic feature is its long, upturned bill which is ideal for digging up molluscs, crustaceans and insects from the bottom and bringing them to the surface, where it then makes short work of them. This beak was once thought to be a freak of nature but is now recognised as a functional implement used by the bird in its particular type of fishing. It was also formerly believed that this curved beak restricted the bird's vision in flight, but this, too, has been shown to be erroneous. In fact the avocet flies with its head dipping downwards, looking beyond the tip of its bill and turning its head to the right and left, so that it has all-round vision with no blind spots.

Like other birds, the avocet has developed a number of ruses to assist it in the struggle for survival. The eggs, for example, are camouflaged in such a way that they blend completely with their surroundings and are pear-shaped rather than oval, which prevents them from rolling out of the nest. The inside of the egg is a beautiful porcelain-white, which means that when they hatch the fragments of shell are visible from afar and draw attention to the nest. The avocet is, therefore, quick to remove these remains as soon as the chicks are hatched. The young instinctively make themselves as inconspicuous as possible, either flattening themselves into the ground with their eyes half closed or keeping their body constantly turned into the sun in order to cast as little shadow as possible. While the eggs and nestlings make

Far right a coot's nest containing six eggs. The coot builds its nest to suit the location and some constructed on water have been strong enough to support a man

Below the dabchick always chooses to nest in areas well concealed by vegetation and where the waters are relatively still

maximum use of camouflage the adult birds provide still further protection by doing all they can to attract the attention of any potential enemy. They are constantly on the alert and at the first sign of danger will take to the air, emitting a loud whistle, like the sound of a flute.

It seems incongruous that the avocet should have such a conspicuous black-and-white plumage when it is surrounded by so many enemies who would delight in its eggs. But this colouring is, in fact, a fairly sophisticated device for deceiving these very predators: the avocet will rise in flight while the creature is still quite some distance from the nest, but its striking plumage draws attention to it and away from the eggs and chicks. It does not, however, rely solely on its colouring to attract

Following page a crowd of coot trying to launch themselves into the air. Despite beating their wings to reach a particular speed they have great difficulty in rising from the water

Below a group of coot fighting over territory as the mating season approaches

Facing page, top left a black tern approaches its nest, built on floating plants, as a chick waits eagerly for food

Centre newly hatched black tern chicks in the nest

Bottom a newly born moorhen chick beside the remaining eggs, as yet unhatched

Below the tern with its beautiful plumage and also, just visible, a newly hatched chick. The tern lays its eggs in a hollow which it makes in the ground by removing sand and stones

attention in such circumstances, but will also abandon its habitual composure and perform wild antics in the air. It soars skywards, drops suddenly on to the water, spreads its wings and launches itself upwards again. All the predator can do is watch in amazement, but this is sufficient for the avocet's purpose as it has held the eyes of the enemy long enough to enable the chicks to seek refuge.

The marsh community also includes a number of birds which are very able swimmers. One of these is the great crested grebe (*Podiceps cristatus*), distinguished by a red band round its neck and two tufts of black feathers on the top of its head. It has a suspicious nature, swimming through the marsh almost completely submerged, with only its head and the top of its neck protruding from the water. At the slightest hint of danger it dives under the water and disappears. The observer will have to scan the surface patiently for some time before he sees it re-emerge a hundred metres or more away.

If it is allowed to swim undisturbed, the great crested grebe will be seen to dive at fairly regular intervals in search of fish and frogs. From time to time it will reappear on the surface, after a seemingly interminable dive, with a fish held firmly but still struggling in its beak.

During the mating season the grebe indulge in the most elaborate courtship rituals. After presenting themselves by bowing and dipping their beaks, they spread their wings and assume what is known as the 'cat' position, which serves to indicate that they are sexually aroused. The ceremony then proceeds with the male diving and then, as soon as he re-emerges, bowing again to his mate who accepts the compliment quietly. They then exchange marsh grasses to seal their partnership.

The grebe builds its own nest on the surface of the water. It appears to be nothing more than a pile of broken reeds and grasses accumulated by the wind, but it is, in fact, a sophisticated piece of engineering. It is built in the form of a floating raft firmly anchored to a clump of reeds to prevent the nest drifting away but

allowing it to rise and fall with the level of the water, so that there is no risk of it being submerged. The female lays her eggs, usually two or three in number, in the centre of this floating bed and both parents incubate them. In order to enable them both to leave the nest in search of food at the same time, the adult birds have developed an original and ingenious way of protecting the nest: they cover the eggs with rotting grass. This serves not only to hide the eggs but also to keep them warm and allow the process of incubation to continue.

The young grebe are able to swim within only hours of hatching and after a few days they can dive and remain under the water for lengthy periods. But they cannot swim as well as the adult birds and when they have to travel some distance the parents will often carry them on their backs. When the grebe have to dive to escape danger the young are able to dive with their parents and remain submerged for as long as necessary.

Another member of the grebe family which can swim very ably on the water and even better under it is the dabchick (*Podiceps ruficollis*). It is smaller than the great crested grebe and its plumage is dark, with the exception of the neck feathers which are reddish in colour. It builds its nest and camouflages its eggs in the same way as the great crested grebe but does employ an original method of teaching its young to fish: the parents bring food to the nest and feed the chicks during the first few days only, then they leave food, such as molluscs, insects and small fish, on the surface of the water near the nest and wait for the young to dip into the water and fish it out again. The impatient, hungry chicks are not particularly appreciative of this but it is a quick and effective method of training them to be independent.

The coot (*Fulica atra*) also spends much of its time swimming on the surface of the water. It, too, has to be able to dive, as the grasses on which it feeds are generally found beneath the surface. As it isn't as skilful an underwater swimmer as the grebe or dabchick it cannot remain submerged for as long, so when danger threatens it doesn't dive in search of refuge but prefers to take to the air. It has difficulty in actually taking off from the water as it literally has to run along the surface, sending up clouds of spray and beating its wings furiously until it has gathered sufficient speed to lift it into the air. This struggle to take off certainly makes the

84

coot appear rather ungainly, but it has characteristics and abilities not displayed by other birds. Above all it has inordinately possessive instincts. Males can often be seen fighting over a female or even over territory. Its legs are somewhat different from those of other aquatic birds in that they have lobes on the toes which act as paddles and enable the bird to swim very fast.

The coot adapts the construction of its nest to the requirements of its location. For instance it can build a traditional nest in the bank vegetation; or it may build a floating or anchored nest, depending on the depth of water (nests weighing up to a thousand kilogrammes and capable of supporting the weight of a man have been found); or again it may build in the branches of a tree or perch the nest on a clump of reeds.

The moorhen (*Gallinula chloropus*) is very similar to the coot though it is smaller and its beak is not white but red. Its nest is generally a platform made from aquatic vegetation, hidden among the reeds and marsh plants, and is built by both parents. The moorhen is solitary rather than gregarious like the coot. Other birds which belong to this family, the rails, are the purple gallinule (*Porphyrio porphyrio*), found only rarely in Europe, and the water-rail (*Rallus aquaticus*), which is excessively timid and doesn't often appear in the open.

The marsh skies seem bare and empty if there is not a tern somewhere in evidence wheeling over the water and then suddenly swooping down on some unlucky fish. Of all the aquatic bird the terns are among the most elegant and agile in the air.

The common tern (*Sterna hirundo*) and the little tern (*S. albifrons*) have long, thin beaks and their wings and tail are pointed. The top of their head is black and they both have short legs. But the beak and legs of the common tern are reddish, while those of the little tern are yellow. These birds generally nest on open, pebbly or sandy ground near water. The female digs out a hollow for the nest and lines it with pebbles to provide camouflage for the eggs. She generally lays three or four eggs and incubates them herself, while the male brings food.

The black tern (*Chlidonias niger*) and whiskered tern (*C. hybrida*) are similar in appearance to the common and little terns, though slightly

Although skilful in the air and able to withstand strong sea winds, gulls sometimes prefer the calmer marsh environment

darker in colour. They also fly and fish in the same way, swooping rapidly down on to the water to catch their prey. Unlike the first two terns, however, they prefer to nest on floating plants such as water-lilies rather than solid ground. They build their nests by piling together small twigs and plant debris. Once the eggs hatch, the parents find it difficult to keep the hungry chicks satisfied. It is a continuous cycle: the parent arrives with food, pauses for an instant above the nest to ensure he has found the right one, then lands gently on it or on a water-lily leaf and puts the food into the widest-open and by implication the hungriest beak.

Gulls, too, display as much skill in the air as the terns. They are sea birds, used to withstanding storm winds, but they sometimes prefer the calm of inland marshes and lakes.

The black-headed gull (*Larus ridibundus*) is frequently found on inland waters. Its feathers moult regularly. When it is young the upper parts of its body are covered with dark patches and the adult bird's head is white in winter and chocolate brown in summer. It is skilled in fishing but is also happy to follow behind the plough and feed on the worms turned over in the earth. The black-headed gull prefers to nest in colonies on open ground near water. These birds have a strong community spirit. If a predator appears he is immediately surrounded by a furious flurry of gulls which will not hesitate to attack him ferociously. It is therefore unwise, even for a man, to approach the colony without adequate protection. As a consequence, other more placid birds will seek to nest near a gull colony in order to benefit from the protection afforded to the territory.

The herring gull (*Larus argentatus*) and the lesser black-headed gull (*L. fuscus*) are also frequent visitors to inland waters and will sometimes nest there.

The Anatidae, a family which includes ducks, geese and swans, are very much aquatic birds and often found in marshy regions. Some European geese such as the greylag goose (*Anser anser*), the white-fronted goose (*A. albifrons*) and the bean goose (*A. fabalis*) pass through southern Europe during migration. The whooper swan (*Cygnus cygnus*), however, does so less frequently and it is even more rare for the mute swan (*C. olor*), which nests in northern Europe, to venture further south than the Alps. But the south of Europe does see a great many species of duck, including the

pintail (*Anas acuta*), the wigeon (*A. penelope*), the gadwall (*A. strepera*), the shoveler (*Spatula clypeata*), the pochard (*Aythya ferina*), the tufted duck (*A. fuligula*), the scaup (*A. marila*), the goldeneye (*Bucephala clangula*), the red-breasted merganser (*Mergus serrator*) and the goosander (*M. merganser*). A number of duck species nest in Italy, including, for example, the teal (*Anas crecca*), the garganey (*A. querquedula*), the ferruginous duck (*Aythya nyroca*), the red-crested pochard (*Netta rufina*) and the white-headed duck (*Oxyura leucocephala*). The last two are found only in the very south of the country and on the islands.

The most common species of duck in southern Europe is the mallard, which is also a favourite game bird. The mallard is a smallish duck, approximately 60 cm in length, with an attractive plumage: in winter the head and upper parts of the neck of the adult male are a beautiful green, with a white collar separating them from the rest of the feathers which are themselves various shades of greys and browns. During winter they band together in colonies containing twenty to fifty birds, or sometimes even as many as a hundred. The mallard is most active during the hours of twilight, when it will swim among the marsh vegetation, where the water is shallowest, every so often plunging its head, neck and breast into the water and leaving only its tail in the air. In this position it can use its bill to search the muddy bed for food.

During spring, from the end of March to June, the male is monogamous. Together he and his mate build the nest. He collects the material, mainly reeds and other marsh grasses, and the female arranges it in a pile, hollowing out the centre by rotating her body. Then she

Facing page, top a flock of herring gulls in flight

Bottom ducks, such as these mallards, are found on marshlands throughout the world

Below starlings often migrate in such large flocks that they darken the sky as they pass

puts the finishing touches to it, lining it with soft material and finally with a few feathers which she plucks from her breast. She lays a number of eggs and incubates them herself. During this period the male moults and prefers to remain hidden in the thick of the reeds.

The young mallards, like ducklings in general, are nidifugous: in other words shortly after hatching they will leave the nest and follow the mother, even into the water where they quickly learn to swim. To begin with they do not stray far from her and if she senses danger she will quickly gather them under her wings and guide them to safety among the reeds. Sometimes if the menace is immediate and there is no time to seek refuge the chicks will dive beneath the water, leaving only their beaks above the surface to enable them to breathe. The marsh is also the home of numerous smaller birds, from the brightly hued kingfisher (*Alcedo atthis*) to the starling (*Sturnus vulgaris*), which will sometimes completely fill the marsh skies during the migration seasons.

The marshlands are also the habitat of numerous other species of passerines, such as the reed warbler (*Acrocephalus scirpaceus*), the marsh warbler (*A. palustris*), the sedge warbler (*A. schoenobaenus*), the aquatic warbler (*A. paludicola*), Cetti's warbler (*Cettia cetti*), Temminck's grasshopper warbler (*Locustella lanceolata*), the great reed warbler (*Acrocephalus arundinaceus*) and the reed bunting (*Emberiza schoeniclus*).

The reed warbler and great reed warbler are identical apart from their size, with the latter being the larger as its name would suggest, and both are skilled in the art of nest building. The nests are more or less cylindrical, like a deep cup, and are made from grass, twigs and other

Above, left the long-eared owl is a typical marsh bird. It hunts during the hours of darkness and twilight

Above, right the fish eagle feeds on fish, which it will swoop down to catch, and also on food which it forces other birds to surrender

material carefully interwoven and firmly secured to a clump of reeds. Flexible so that they will not be damaged as the reeds bend in the wind, they are lined with mosses, roots and finally with the flowers of marsh plants. It is hardly surprising that the cuckoo chooses to lay its eggs in these nests. Unfortunately the young cuckoo is small but aggressive and quite capable of ousting the rightful inhabitants.

The bearded tit (*Panurus biarmicus*) is another reed dweller which displays considerable skill in the construction of its nest, which is almost spherical in shape with a small entrance hole. The birds build near to one another in a bed of reeds, lining the inside of the nest with flower petals and a few feathers. The greatest ability in this field is, however, undoubtedly shown by the penduline tit (*Remiz pendulinus*) which builds a flask-shaped nest with one or two small entrances and suspended from the branch of a tree. It uses fine grasses, fibres and hairs which it weaves into a thick mat. To this it attaches small balls of down from various plants glued together by saliva and held by threads. It then lines the inside with pappus, hair or fluff.

Special mention must be made of the birds of prey. In many places their numbers have been severely diminished by over-zealous hunters. These birds do, in fact, fulfil a useful function in that they help to dispose of weak or sick creatures and thus allow the fittest to survive. Typical daytime raptors are the marsh harriers (*Circus aeruginosus*) which are, however, now relatively rare. But the marsh may also be the home of Montagu's harrier (*Circus pygargus*) and the osprey (*Pandion haliaetus*). The European raptors which prefer the marsh environment, the spotted eagle (*Aquila clanga*) and the lesser-spotted eagle (*A. pomarina*), are found only in eastern Europe.

The short-eared owl (*Asio flammeus*) and the long-eared owl (*A. otus*) are found widely in central and northern Europe. They are night predators which prefer wetlands because they are ideal as hunting-grounds.

The mammal community of the marshes is much smaller and less colourful than the bird kingdom. It does, however, include the wild boar (*Sus scrofa*), a strong creature practically without enemies. The boar is not, strictly speaking, a marsh creature as it also lives in completely different environments, but if there is a marsh of any sort near its home it will certainly find its way there to wallow in the mud. This explains why boars are found commonly in regions with extensive marshlands such as parts of the Tyrrhenian coast, in particular the Tenuta di S.Rossore, the Trappola marshes and the Circeo National Park. Fallow deer (*Dama dama*) are also found in these regions and occasionally their antlers can be seen emerging from among the marsh grasses.

There is one mammal associated exclusively with aquatic environments – the otter (*Lutra lutra*). A predator which lives solely on a diet of fish, it is consequently regarded as an enemy of fisherman and the species has been almost completely destroyed. There are other, smaller European mammals which are much more common, such as the water-vole (*Arvicola terrestris*), the harvest mouse (*Micromys minutus*) and in some places the wild rabbit (*Oryctolagus cuniculus*), which will pepper the shores and banks of the marsh with its burrows.

Facing page an unusual photograph of a pack of young wild boars. They are often to be seen wallowing in marshland mud

Below an aquatic environment is necessary for the common otter, which feeds mainly on fish

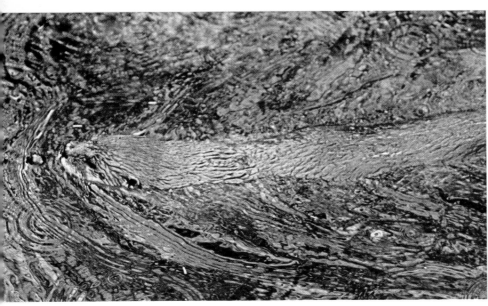

Chapter Four
The World's Wetlands

*Marshlands can vary widely in their flora and fauna
according to the way in which they were originally formed, the climate
which prevails in them and whether or not they are permanent or seasonal. This chapter lists
and describes the characteristics of major marshlands throughout the world
and shows how their value as unique sources of information on plant and animal life
will be lost for ever, unless national parks and reservations
are created to protect them.*

Facing page
An expanse of waterlogged land in Florida, with tall
trees and, in the foreground, marsh samphires

Marshes vary according to the way in which they were formed – for example coastal or inland marshes – to the climate and also to whether they are permanent or seasonal. These various features result in turn in appreciable differences in the flora and fauna. Despite the fact that many marshes have been drained there are still numerous wet regions available to the naturalist or to anyone who is interested. Whatever their size, these areas are generally valuable sources of information on animal and plant life as they exhibit characteristics which are not and cannot be reproduced elsewhere. Many more of these regions are, however, likely to be lost for all time unless national parks and reservations are created to protect them.

Europe

ITALY

Of the European marshlands Italy has some of the most valuable to wildlife. In the Piedmont region thriving mountain marshes, located in the area round the source of the Belbo, consist of expanses of wetland interspersed with numerous semi-stagnant tarns. The vegetation comprises mainly alders, poplars and willows. Lake Candia has a large area of reeds inhabited by ducks and wading birds, while the rice fields between Novara and Vercelli are the home of many water birds including a variety of herons (the night heron, the blue-grey heron, the egret and the squacco), moorhens, terns and some kingfishers. One of the largest heronries in Piedmont lies in a magnificent wood of willows and poplars near Crescentino, where blue-grey herons, night herons and egrets all nest.

The Lombardy marshes of Provaglio d'Iseo, or more precisely those which have escaped drainage, contain many marsh grasses and water-lillies, while little bitterns, mallards, garganeys and teal nest in the reeds. A prodigious animal community inhabits the region round Lake Como, especially in the marshes on the Spagna plain and around Lake Mezzola. Species include reed warblers, herons, little bitterns, geese, moorhens, mallards and other ducks; otters are sometimes seen.

Another region of considerable interest is the Venice lagoon, where from Chioggia to Jesolo

Below a marsh pool at Bolgheri, in Tuscany, the home of large numbers of ducks and herons and where flamingoes and black-winged stilt are also sighted from time to time

ducks, grebe and even cormorants and coot are found in the parts nearest the sea, where the tides bring constant changes of water. The inner reaches are inhabited by waders such as egrets, herons, plovers and snipe.

The Po valley marshland covers an area of approximately 17,000 hectares, though originally it extended to more than 300 sq km. The flora includes marsh samphires and zostera, the fauna, ducks, herons, egrets, terns, black-winged stilt and avocets.

The marshes found along the Adriatic coast between the mouth of the Po and the Ravenna pine woods are among the best preserved in Italy. The large bird community includes various heron and anatid species.

In Tuscany, the region from Migliarono to San Rossore encompasses the marshlands at the mouths of the Arno and the Serchio and also woodland lakes. The World Wildlife Fund Sanctuary at Bolgheri includes duck, herons, egrets, lapwings, moorhens, coot and snipe. Flamingoes, black-winged stilt and glossy ibis are other occasional visitors to the region.

GREAT BRITAIN

The coastal flats and marshes, as well as estuaries, are particularly important, not only for nesting birds but also for North Eurasian waders on passage migration and as a terminal over-wintering ground for wildfowl breeding in Arctic Russia, Scandinavia and Iceland.

The large estuaries, such as Morecambe Bay, the Wash, Solway Firth, and the Dee and Ribble, are internationally important as a wintering ground for nearly thirty species of waders. Morecambe Bay, with its intertidal flats, supports the largest wintering flocks of waders, especially oystercatchers, curlew, god-wits, knot, dunlin and sanderling, with good number of grey plover. The Wash, which is the second most important coastal site, is also significant for wildfowl. The sand, silt and mudflats provide food for wintering flocks of brent geese, pinkfeet and wigeon. The sand-banks provide a habitat for seals; common seals breed there, while both common and grey seals haul out on the banks. The Ribble supports large numbers of wildfowl on its large sandflats, especially pinkfeet and waders such

Below the Comacchio Valley in Romagna is literally covered with plants such as the white water-lily, which grows on ponds and slow-moving waters

as knot and dunlin. The Dee estuary also has large numbers of wildfowl, especially pintail, shelduck, scaup, scoter and golden eye. The bar-tailed godwit is a feature of wintering wader populations and some of the smaller estuaries also support high densities in the winter, including rare species. The Beaulieu estuary, for example, has spotted redshank.

The most important wildfowl wintering sites are the Ouse Washes. Here the meadow grasslands are flooded during the winter and provide the best inland area for dabbling ducks, with huge overwintering flocks of wigeon, pintail and significant numbers of Bewick's swans. Other important winter wildfowl localities are Loch Leven, Firth of Forth, Gomarty Firth, Caerlaverock and the Stour estuary (Essex).

Several of the above coastal marshes, such as Morecambe Bay and Solway, are important for nesting birds during the spring and summer. Saltmarsh-nesting black-headed gulls are increasing on marshes in Kent and Hampshire, while on the north Kent marshes, which support a few nesting pochard and pintail, the reclaimed grazing marshes behind the sea wall have been colonized by a number of the same species. Minsmere, in Suffolk, has many breeding duck including gadwall; Loch Druidibeg on South Uist, in the Outer Hebrides, has the largest native breeding colony of greylag geese.

Reed swamps occur along the Norfolk Broads, on the north Norfolk coast, at Poole Harbour, Chichester Harbour and at Stodmarsh, in Kent. All provide habitats for nesting species such as marsh harrier, bittern, bearded tit and quantities of reed warbler.

Certain reed and osier beds are especially important as roosts for swallows and martins on migration. Such places in the Ouse Washes are used by sand martins, while coastal reed beds in Somerset, at Slapton in Devon, and in Norfolk and Suffolk are similarly used by autumn concentrations of reed and sedge warblers.

Left, top oystercatchers nest in coastal regions throughout almost the entire world.

Centre flamingoes on the Fournelet pool in the Camargue, France

Bottom a scene on the Etang de Vaccarès in the Camargue, with flamingoes in the foreground sifting the water for food.

Above sand dunes on the Coto Doñana, Spain, a large wildlife reserve with surrounding marshland inhabited by many bird species as well as deer, wild boar and lynx

FRANCE

The best known marsh region in France is undoubtedly the Camargue. It extends over an area of 540 sq km, about half of which is covered, as it always has been, with brackish marshes and pools of varying degrees of salinity. Part of this area has been made into a national park. The flora and fauna are varied but, perhaps most importantly, it is the only place in Europe where flamingoes (on average more than 10,000 of them) nest regularly, building strange, crater-shaped nests in the mud. Other species common in the Camargue are avocets, pratincoles, squacco herons, penduline and bearded tits, terns, herons and raptors, such as kites, kestrels, marsh harriers and Bonelli's eagle. Summer visitors to the region include the roller, the hoopoe and the bee-eater.

SPAIN

The region of most interest is the Coto Doñana Reserve and surrounding marshlands, an area of some 840 sq km at the mouth of the Guadalquivir. Flamingoes nest there and it is the home of numerous other birds, including some rare species: cranes, spoonbills, glossy ibis, avocets, black-winged stilt, purple gallinules, storks, herons, large numbers of duck, greylag geese, short-eared owls and Egyptian vultures.

SARDINIA

The island contains fairly extensive marshes, in particular salt or brackish coastal pools, the home of colonies of flamingo numbering several thousand birds and also of purple gallinule, rarely found in other parts.

THE NETHERLANDS

The island of Texel has several expanses of marshland which have been declared protected zones. In all, 117 different birds nest there, selecting the environment and degree of salinity which best suits them. They include avocets, spoonbills, plovers, lapwings, mallards, terns, shovelers, coot, greylag geese, pochards, snipe and gulls.

SWITZERLAND

There are still about 200 hectares of completely undeveloped land at the source of the Rhône on Lake Geneva. A fairly large number of animals, including wild boar and otters, live among the thick bushes and reeds; 88 bird species are known to nest there regularly and many more migratory birds stop there temporarily. On the eastern shores of the lake at Neuchâtel an area of reed-covered marsh about 500 m wide and 10 km long is a major European nesting ground for aquatic birds.

Above, left some of the varied plant life on the marshes at the mouth of the Guadalquivir, Spain

Above, right mosaic formed by cracks in parched marshland in the Camargue, France

SWEDEN

The Muddus National Park contains expanses of tundra inhabited by numerous aquatic birds. A national park has been created round the lakes at Padjelanta.

AUSTRIA

On the Hungarian border there is a large marshy area in the Neusiedler reserve inhabited by numerous bird species, such as spoonbills, white herons, grebe, geese and ducks. During the migration season there might be more than 100,000 geese in view at any one time. Other regions worth mentioning are the Marchegg Nature Reserve, where cormorants, storks and night herons are found, Lake Lacke, the bed of the river Enns, the Furtner Teich Nature Reserve, one of the first places to be used for the observation of migratory birds, and the artificial lake and surrounding bog at Kops Stansee.

POLAND

Many aquatic birds, including cranes, storks, swans and raptors, live in the marshlands in the Bielowieza Forest National Park. Other parks of interest are at Kampinos, where there are herons and cranes, Czerwone Bagno, Jezioro Lukniany and Torfowisko pod Zielencem.

NORWAY

There is little wetland in Norway apart from the fjord valleys, where a healthy growth of flora can be found. Geese and duck are among the migratory water birds but more can be found in the Fokstumyra Nature Reserve, the Øvre Dividal National Park and other wildlife sanctuaries.

DENMARK

Geese, terns, swans and ducks are frequent visitors to the Tipperne and Klaegbauken Reserve in the Ringkøbing fjord and there is also a reserve at Hansted where ducks, golden plovers and roe deer are found.

WEST GERMANY

Regions of interest are the Einkircher marshes on Lake Constance, Wedel marshes and Elb estuary round Hamburg. Ducks, terns, lapwings and ruffs are found on Lake Dümmer near Osnabrück and ducks, herons, bitterns, terns, gulls and marsh harriers on the Federsee near Biberach. Also worthy of mention are Gelting Birk and the Schleswig-Holstein lakes, the Grosser Rohrpfuhl in West Berlin and Die Lucie in Lower Saxony, where cranes are found. The foothills of the Bavarian Alps also have considerable marshlands.

HUNGARY

The Kisbalaton Reserve on Lake Balaton is the home of numerous bird species. Also of importance are Lake Velence and the Feher Reserve on the lake of the same name, though in fact a large proportion of the Hungarian puszta consists of lakes and waterlogged land.

CZECHOSLOVAKIA

The Biskupice Reserve has a large bird community, including the cormorant. In addition there are marshes at Lednice near Brno, a reserve at Mrtvy Luh and marshes along the course of the Danube.

RUMANIA

The Danube delta and the Razelm lagoon together form one of the largest expanses of marshland in Europe. The enormous variety of birds includes pelicans, herons, ducks, swans, coot, curlews and stone curlews, bee-eaters and rollers. There are also marshes along the course of the Danube and Lake Snagov.

BULGARIA

The Vitoča National Park contains some interesting bog-land. In addition there are the Burgas, Mandra and Atansovo lakes, some bird reserves on the Danube, the Srebarna Park, where herons, swans and pelicans can be found, and the Ropotamo Park, which is the home of greylag geese, deer, wild boar and roe deer.

YUGOSLAVIA

Spoonbills, pelicans, glossy ibis, storks and great white herons can be seen throughout the country. Regions of particular interest are Lake Scutari, where there are pelicans, Lake Prespa, the Neretva delta, the confluence of the Danube and the Drava and of the Danube and the Sava, the Plitvička Jezera National Park with its numerous lakes, and Hutovo Blato, Obedska Bara and Monostorski Riitovi.

GREECE

One of the largest bird communities to inhabit a river mouth in Europe is found in the delta of the Maritza where ducks, coot, waders, raptors, herons, including the great white heron, spoonbills, storks, pelicans, stone curlews, rollers, bee-eaters, pratincoles and black-winged stilt live. Important, too, are the mouths of the rivers Nestos and Axiòs, Lakes Prespa and Giannina, the Missolungi lagoon and the Pỳgros marshes.

FINLAND

The extensive inner 'lake district' of Finland, characterized by a network of archipelagoes, attracts large numbers of nesting waterfowl, while the wet coastal regions are visited by seabirds such as the Caspian tern and black guillemot. Meadowland made highly fertile by flooding rivers produces a vast variety of wild flora and in the north substantial yields of cloudberries are harvested among the sphagnum swamps, also populated by plagues of mosquitoes.

SOVIET UNION

The Volga delta encloses an impressive area of marshland. The varied plant community of the Astrakan Reserve includes in particular the Indian lotus. This reserve is also the home of numerous aquatic birds such as herons, grebe, pelicans, cormorants, geese and ducks. There are also marshes along the banks of the main rivers, the Volga, the Dnieper, the Don and the Ural.

For about two months in the summer the vast Siberian tundra is alive with swans, geese, ducks, sandpipers, turnstones, snipe, curlews and black- and red-throated divers. At the end of August these migratory birds fly off. The low-lying marshy plains of the Samarkand are inhabited by wading birds such as herons.

South East Asia

Along the majority of the coasts of the Indo-China and Malaysian peninsulas and on the islands in the Philippines and Indonesian archipelagos there are extensive mangrove swamps, which are the home of birds, such as wood storks and kingfishers, snakes, strange creatures like the giant crab and reptilian fish.

The Indo-Chinese peninsula has extensive rice plantations, particularly in the Mekong basin. Although this land is under cultivation it provides an ideal habitat for many bird species, such as ducks, ardeids, water-pheasants and purple gallinules, and also for reptiles and amphibians. In addition there are large tracts of marshland at the mouths of the Irrawaddy and Menam rivers and that of the Red River.

Other areas worth mentioning are Lake Inle in Burma, the Angkor National Park in Cambodia, the water catchment park in Singapore, and the parks at Paudan and Krankji.

Right, top a pair of pelicans, birds which live in shallow waters and generally nest among the reeds

Bottom the Indian wood stork is still fairly common on marshland throughout South-East Asia

Following pages the Indian or unicorn rhinoceros is found on marshland in various nature-reserves

Indian Subcontinent

The Kazirange National Park on the banks of the Brahmaputra contains expanses of wetland in which there is a rich and varied animal life including rhinoceroses, marsh deer, tigers, elephants and water-buffalo, as well as many bird species such as wood storks, ibis, cranes, ducks and herons.

There is also a large bird community on the Bharatpur Reserve, where kingfishers, wood storks, ibis, cranes, herons, night herons and ducks are all found, and in eastern Bengal an important reserve at Jadalpara, where the marshlands are inhabited by rhinoceroses. There are also parks at Taroba in India, where crocodiles and tigers are found, at Chitawan in

Nepal, the home of rhinoceroses, elephants, tigers, crocodiles, gavials, etc., at Sukla Phanta again in Nepal, where there are marsh deer, tigers and elephants, and at Chittagong in Bangladesh, where there are tigers and deer. Tigers and crocodiles also live in the vast marshy regions at the mouth of the Ganges and the Brahmaputra. There are extensive mangrove swamps on the Gulf of Bengal at the south-eastern tip of the Indian peninsula and along the coast between Karachi and Bombay.

Far East

The Noda Sagiyama Park in Japan is inhabited by a huge colony of great white herons. There

Above, left the tiger, drastically reduced by hunting both in India and on the Indo-Chinese peninsula

Above, right the marsh deer from northern India has an impervious coat and large hooves which make it eminently suitable for life in the marshes

are marshes on Hokkaido islands, which are the home of the Japanese crane (*Grus japonensis*), and in the Nikko, Shiretoko and Akan Parks. In China the Yangtze Kiang is flanked by vast rice fields with an interesting bird community which includes the brightly hued mandarin duck (*Aix galericulata*).

Australasia and Oceania

Mangrove swamps similar to those found in South East Asia are also to be seen on the coasts of New Guinea and northern Australia. The river estuaries in this region are inhabited by salt-water crocodiles (*Crocodylus porosus*), which can be up to 9 m in length. A common bird in this continent is the black swan (*Cygnus atratus*), which lives in large colonies in the wetlands in Tasmania and on Lake George near Canberra.

The most interesting wetland regions here are the lower reaches of the Murray river and Lakes Alexandrina, Albert and Coorong, where black swans, pelicans and ducks are found; Lake Hattah, the home of pelicans, ducks, herons, cormorants, avocets and kangaroos; the Macquairie marshes in New South Wales, where there are herons, spoonbills, cormorants, geese, black ducks, Australian ibis, bitterns and coot; Lake Bulloo and the marshes along the lower stretches of numerous rivers in the north of Australia, such as the Victoria, the Adelaide and the Mary. Also worthy of mention are Coburg Park, a mangrove swamp inhabited by herons, ibis, swans and ducks, and Mount Field National Park in Tasmania, the home of duck-billed platypus and kangaroos.

In New Zealand there are marshlands in the Egmont and Abel Tasman national parks.

Africa

SUDAN
Along the banks of the Nile in the south there are vast tracts of marshland on which papyrus, reeds, aquatic grasses and water-lilies grow.

ETHIOPIA
The Ethiopian plateau contains numerous marshes and bogs which are the home of migratory duck such as the wigeon and seasonal species including the *Anas ondulata*, the Egyptian goose and the wattled crane.

SENEGAL
The Niokolo Koba National Park is the home of elephants, hippopotami, wart-hogs, riverhogs, crocodiles and numerous bird species and there are heron colonies on the Djoval Nature Reserve.

MALI
There are vast expanses of marshland along the banks of the Niger, while Lake Debo is the habitat of waders, ducks, black-tailed godwits and numerous other species.

IVORY COAST, GHANA AND BENIN
The Bouna reserve in the Ivory Coast contains elephants and hippopotami. In Ghana there is a mangrove swamp on the coast at the mouth

Above a stretch of waterlogged land in the Angkor national park, Cambodia

of the Volta and in Benin the National Park at the mouth of the Pendjari is inhabited by elephants, hippopotami, antelopes, wart-hogs, crowned cranes, herons and marabou storks.

NIGERIA

There are mangrove swamps scattered all along the coast, in particular around the Niger delta. The region around Lake Chad is also of interest and there is a reserve at Yankari in which elephants, hippopotami, antelopes and crocodiles are found.

CHAD

Lake Chad, situated in a large basin, is itself comprised of two basins; both are shallow – the north basin rarely more than 8 m deep and the south 5 m – but subject to rising in particular years. When this occurs, the south basin over-flows into the lowlands of the main basin and inundates surrounding land. There are also swampy shores where the Komadugu Yobe and Shari rivers flow into the lake from the south-west and south-east. From time to time there have been fears that the lake, particularly the north basin, will dry up, due to sand deposits, vegetation growth and evaporation.

Various plants abound in the marshy areas with an abundance of papyrus. There are Wildlife parks at Zakouma and Manda, while the Rhine-Ouadi Achim Reserve, opened in 1969, is the biggest nature reserve in Africa.

CAMEROUN

Here there is a National Park at Waza on the shores of Lake Chad in which elephants, wart-hogs, pelicans, crowned cranes, ducks, geese, gazelles and marabous can be seen. Mangrove swamps are found along the Atlantic coast.

Central Africa

ZAIRE

The marshlands of the Congo basin include the area around Lake Maidombe (formerly Leopold II), which is permanently under

Facing page marshland scene in Siberia at the beginning of spring

Right, top the majestic posture of the Australian black swan as it sits on its nest

Right, bottom Johnson's crocodile, characterized by its long thin head, is found in rivers and marshes in northern Australia

water, and that around Lake Tumba. In addition the Upemba and Albert National Parks are the home of cormorant and marabou.

RUANDA

The areas of interest here are Lake Kivu (which is mainly in Zaire) and the Kagera National Park in which hippopotami and river-hogs can be found.

UGANDA

Worth noting are the northern shores of Lake Victoria, Lakes Mobutu Sese Seko (formerly Albert), on the borders with Zaire, and Idi Amin Dada (formerly Edward), the Kabalega Falls (formerly Murchison Falls) National Park, where elephants, hippopotami, black rhinoceroses, crocodiles and crowned cranes live among the papyrus. The elephant and hippopotamus are again found in the Queen Elizabeth park and on the Toro Game Reserve.

KENYA

Again the shores of Lake Victoria are of interest, as are the Great Rift Valley Lakes, namely Lake Baringo, the home of crocodiles and many bird species, Lake Naivasha, again with a large bird community, and Lake Magadi. The bird species which can be seen here include herons, pelicans, eagles, kingfishers, jacanas and ducks. Lake Nakuru is particularly interesting as its waters are extremely alkaline and it is the home of a large flamingo colony. Flamingoes are also found on Lake Elmenteita, while the Tsavo National Park contains the magnificent Mzima springs. The Aberdare National Park has mountain bog-land expanses and hippopotami inhabit the game reserve at Meru.

TANZANIA

Of interest are Lake Tanganyika, the Lake Manyara National Park, where elephants, black rhinoceroses, hippopotami, pelicans and flamingoes can be found, and Lakes Eyasi, Natron and Rukwa. In addition there are marshes in the Kilombero Valley and in the region to the west of Tabora. Rhinoceroses, elephants and hippopotami live in the Ruaha park and there are reserves at Ngorongoro, Uwanda and Katavi.

Facing page the Moluccan ibis is found only in the wetlands of Molucca, New Guinea, Australia and Tasmania

Below Kabalega Falls valley, on the upper reaches of the Nile in Uganda, shelters many animals including elephants, hippopotami and crocodiles

ZAMBIA

Lakes Mweru and Bangweulu are surrounded by marshland and there are reserves at Lukanga Valley (elephants, hippopotami, crocodiles and black rhinoceroses), Mweru (elephants, hippopotami, river-hogs and wart-hogs), Sambu (elephants, hippopotami and wart-hogs) and Lunga and Kasanga (papyrus plantations, elephants and hippopotami).

RHODESIA

There are National Parks at Mushandike, where terns, egrets and herons can be seen, and at Chimanimani, which is the home of many bird species. Elephants, black rhinoceroses, crocodiles, hippopotami, river-hogs and many bird species are found on the Mana Pools Game Reserve.

MOZAMBIQUE

The hippopotamus and crocodile inhabit the marshlands and rivers of Mozambique and lizards and other reptiles are also plentiful. Among the many snakes are cobras, pythons, puff adders and vipers.

There are a number of game reserves, of which the Gorongoza National Park, home of hippopotami, elephants, rhinoceroses, pelicans, spoonbills, cranes and egrets, is one of the largest in the world.

SOUTH AFRICA

Antelope and many species of birds inhabit the Jonker's Hoek Nature Reserve and goliath herons and flamingoes in the Barberspan Reserve. The Saint Lucia mangrove forest is inhabited by hippopotami, crocodiles, pelicans, herons and avocets, while river-hogs and crocodiles live in the Umfolozi mangroves.

U.S.A.

If one particular American region is to be selected as an outstanding example of marshland, it must be the Everglades in Florida. The Everglades proper is a vast area of southern Florida, part of which is a national park. Shallow water flows over the dead flatlands from Lake Okeechobee for 161 km to Florida Bay in a 'river' which is 80 km wide and 152 mm deep. As the water filters through the Everglades to the sea it produces a great variety of wet conditions from saw grass swamp and cypress swamp, which is very wet during the rainy season, to mangrove swamp and saline marshes on the seaward fringes in Florida Bay and the Gulf of

Facing page, top a goliath heron, found on tropical marshland in Africa

Top right the black-and-white kingfisher on a papyrus branch on Lake Naivasha, Kenya

Bottom a colony of pelicans fishing on Lake Nakuru, Kenya

Below flamingoes nesting on the Ngorongoro reserve in Tanzania. In Europe they are mostly found at the mouth of the Guadalquivir river, Spain, and in the Camargue, France

Mexico. This area supports an enormous wealth of wildlife of all kinds.

The rivers contain fish such as gar pike, many alligators and pond-tortoises and mammals such as manatees, the swamps contain white-tailed deer and smaller mammals such as opossums, racoons and otters.

There are about three hundred species of birds in the Everglades including many characteristic wetland species, while within the Everglades area the refuge at Lake Loxahatchee is significant as a locality for the Everglades kite, together with such local specialities as the limpkin and many other marsh birds. In the mangrove swamps there are white ibis, roseate spoonbill, brown and white pelicans, cormorants and ospreys, and in the freshwater swamps there is a different selection of birds with herons, egrets, gallinules, anhingas and raptors, such as the red-shouldered hawk and swallow-tailed kite. Crocodiles occur occasionally in the salt-water swamp.

On the fringes of the Everglades in south-west Florida is the Corkscrew Swamp Sanctuary. This is a wilderness area of old cypress swamp which includes many fine old trees and is protected by the Audubon Society as a breeding site for wood storks and great egrets. There are many other species of egret and heron together with alligators in this area which includes a most interesting wet prairie and a central marsh of saw grass and willow swamp. Red-shouldered hawk also occur here.

Merritt Island, Florida, is a large area of lagoons and marshes surrounding NASA at Cape Kennedy. It is a sanctuary for migrating

Below hippopotami can often be seen bathing in the company of elephants on the banks of the Nile in Uganda

wildfowl and includes such rarities as the southern bald eagle. Alligators are common in the swamps and there are many herons and egrets. Many wildfowl overwinter including pintail, wigeon, teal and the American coot.

Other habitats in the area are mangrove swamp and salt barrens. Pelican Island has a nesting colony together with other seabirds.

Okefenokee Swamp in south Georgia is an old and primitive wetland with alligators and a variety of bird life such as white ibis, sandhill crane and wood duck. The Savannah Wildlife Refuge in South Carolina is an area of abandoned rice fields which form an excellent overwintering site for wildfowl and a good nesting ground for wood duck.

The Mississippi Delta in Louisiana is a wintering ground for thousands of blue and snow geese. As elsewhere in the southern states there are frequent alligators, while sea turtles come ashore there to lay their eggs. Also in Louisiana is Lacassine Wildlife Refuge at Lake Arthur. This is another important waterfowl wintering area with large concentrations of white-fronted geese, and a large population of nesting fulvous tree ducks. In western Tennessee there is an important refuge at Paris where several thousands of ducks and geese overwinter. There are also bald and golden eagles and wild turkey.

There are also extensive marshlands at the mouth of the Mississippi where the native fauna includes bull-frogs (*Rana catesbeiana*) and alligator turtles (*Macrochemys temminckii*) and migratory birds such as geese from the Hudson Bay area who go there to spend the winter.

Below a notable haunt of the Nile crocodile is below the Kabalega Falls in Uganda

Bottom the Mississippi alligator is found in rivers, marshes and pools in the south-eastern states of the USA. It hunts at sunset

Above thick pond vegetation provides ample support for this jacana and her chicks

Facing page, top the scarlet ibis, found on the borders of Venezuela and Brazil, is characterized by its striking red plumage

Bottom the wood or Carolina duck, one of the most attractive birds to be found in wetlands of the North American temperate zones

Central and South America

In Guatemala numerous tropical bird species are found in the Rio Dulce National Park and there are also wetlands of interest in the Petén region in the north of the country and giant grebe (*Podilymbus gigas*) on Lake Atitlán. There are marshes along the Atlantic coast of Nicaragua, Costa Rica, Belize and Honduras and also on the Gulf of Fonseca on the Pacific coast of Honduras. Also worth noting are Lakes Managua and Nicaragua in Nicaragua, the lakes of the Panama canal, some coastal zones, in particular on the Zapata peninsula in Cuba, the Nariva marsh in Trinidad and the salt-marshes of the Bahamas and Andros, on which American flamingoes (*Phoenicopterus ruber*) nest.

COLUMBIA

A rich river alluvium in the lowlands between the northern Andes and Caribbean Sea encourages a multitude of salamanders and frogs as well as the legless amphibian of the family Caecilidae. Similar populations of amphibians are found in the floodplains of the César, San Jorge and Cauca rivers, while along the Magdalena river are a prolific number of American crocodile and some species of cayman. Seasonally flooded swamps bordering the coastal

rivers and tributaries are invaluable as sources of drinking water for livestock during drought, but also produces plagues of mosquitoes. The resultant spreading of malaria has necessitated a large Government investment in an eradication campaign.

VENEZUELA

The areas of interest here are the south-western shores of the Maracaibo lagoon, the Orinoco delta, the plains which are inhabited by scarlet ibis, herons, otters, anacondas and caymans, and some parts of the Henri Pittier National Park, where migratory birds can be seen.

GUYANA

The main marshlands are on the Atlantic coast, where there are mangrove swamps, and along the banks of the major rivers. In Surinam (Dutch Guyana) there are reserves at Wia-Wia, the home of ibis and flamingoes, and at the mouth of the Coppename, where ibis, pelicans and herons are found.

BRAZIL

Vast areas of marshland are found on the banks of the Amazon and its tributaries. During the rainy season the river overflows and floods large areas of the forest. At the river mouth and

along the Atlantic coast there are mangrove swamps. The large plant community includes, among others, *Victoria regia* and various species of *Salvinia* and there is a substantial animal community of caymans, anacondas, tapirs, ant-eaters, capybaras, scarlet ibis, herons, cormorants, etc. On the coast there are marshes in the region known as Pantanal (Mato Grosso on the Bolivian border) and in the Aparados de Serra National Park. On the Jaraguà Nature Reserve there are sizeable bird communities.

ARGENTINA

Both the Chaco and the Corrientes regions have vast expanses of marshland. Also of interest are the southern banks of the River Plate and certain parts of the Pampas, particularly the east where ducks and plovers are found. There are National Parks at Lanin, the home of white herons and Argentinian duck; on the Pilcomayo river, inhabited by caimans, pumas, storks, herons, ducks and greylag geese; and at Chaco, where otters and ducks can be found.

PERU AND BOLIVIA

The regions of interest here are the Andes lakes, such as Lake Titicaca, where the animal community includes ducks, herons, giant coot and flamingoes.

ECUADOR

Dense mangrove forestland borders long stretches of the Pacific coast, notably around the Gulf of Guayaquil and mouth of the Guayas river. Swamp and marsh is also found on the floodplains of most of the country's rivers. The resulting fertility of surrounding land ensures the growth of a number of plant species of economic value, including the balsa tree, from which the world's lightest timber is obtained.

Numerous species of reptiles and amphibians are found in the wetlands but the main wildlife sanctuary is in the San Lorenzo Park, famous for its populations of herons and pelicans.

PARAGUAY

Swampland is found all along the Paraguay river, which bisects the country from north to south and forms borders between Paraguay and Brazil and Argentina. To the west of the river is the vast, flat Chaco Boreal, believed to have been the bed of a prehistoric sea and now featuring a variety of terrain, including swampy lowlands. The largest river in this area is the Pilcomayo, unnavigable and so slow-moving as to cause annual flooding to the surrounding country. All these waterlogged areas attract numerous species of birds, among them the herons, ibis, toucan and black duck.

Above the anaconda lives among water in the huge American tropical forests, often resting on branches overhanging the marsh

Facing page, top typical scene in the Everglades, with a clump of mangroves in the centre

Bottom a pool in the Amazon basin, with marsh vegetation in the foreground

Geographical Index

Page numbers for picture references are in bold type.

Abel Tasman National Park, New Zealand, 105
Aberdare National Park, Kenya, 109
Albert, Lake, Australia, 105
Albert National Park, Zaire, 109
Alexandrina, Lake, Australia, 105
Alps, Switzerland, **32**
Amazon, River, Brazil, 32, 114, **117**
Angkor National Park, Cambodia, 100, **105**
Aparados de Serra National Park, Brazil, 117
Arthur, Lake, USA, 113
Astrakan, Reserve, Soviet Union, 100
Atitlàn, Lake, Guatemala, 114

Balaton, Lake, Hungary, 100
Bangweulu, Lake, Zambia, 111
Barberspan Reserve, South Africa, 111
Baringo, Lake, Kenya, **34**, 109
Belbo, River, Italy, 94
Benin National Park, Nigeria, 107
Bharatpur Reserve, India, 104
Bielowieza Forest National Park, Poland, 99
Biskupice Reserve, Czechoslovakia, 100
Bolgheri World Wild Lfe Fund Sanctuary, Italy, **94**, 95
Bouna Reserve, Ivory Coast, 105
Brahmaputra, River, India, 104

Camargue, France, **11**, 75, **97**, 98, **99**
Candia, Lake, Italy, 94
Cauca, River, Colombia, 114
César, River, Colombia, 114
Chaco, Argentina, 117
Chaco Boreal, Paraguay, 117
Chad, Lake, 107
Chimanimani, Rhodesia, 111
Chitawan, Nepal, 104
Circeo National Park, Italy, 90
Comacchio Valley, Italy, **15**, 57, **95**
Como, Lake, Italy, 94
Constance, Lake, West Germany, 99
Coorong, Lake, Australia, 105
Corkscrew Swamp Sanctuary, Florida, USA, 112
Corrientes, Argentina, 117
Coto Doñana Reserve, Spain, **13**, **98**, 98
Cromarty Firth, Great Britain, 97
Crescentino, Italy, 94

Danube Delta, Rumania, 100
Debo, Lake, Mali, 105
Dee, River, Great Britain, 97
Djoval Nature Reserve, Senegal, 105
Dnieper, River, Soviet Union, 100

Don, River, Soviet Union, 100
Drava, River, Yugoslavia, 100
Dümmer, Lake, West Germany, 99

Edward, Lake, Uganda, 109
Egmont National Park, New Zealand, 105
Elbe Estuary, West Germany, 99
Elmenteita, Lake, Kenya, 109
Ethiopian Plateau, Ethiopia, 105
Eyasi, Lake, Tanzania, 109

Federsee, West Germany, 99
Feher Reserve, Hungary, 100
Firth of Forth, Great Britain, 97
Fokstumyra Nature Reserve, Norway, 99
Furtner Teich Nature Reserve, Austria, 99
Ganges, River, India, 104
Gelting Birk, Lake, West Germany, 99
Geneva, Lake, Switzerland, 98
George, Lake, Australia, 105
Gorongoza National Park, Mozambique, 111
Guadalquivir, River, Spain, **18**, 98, **99**
Guayaquil, Gulf, Ecuador, 117
Guayas, River, Ecuador, 117

Hattah, Lake, Australia, 105
Henri Pittier National Park, Venezuela, 114
Hokkaido Islands, Japan, 105

Idi Amin Dada, Lake, Uganda, 109
Inle, Lake, Burma, 100
Irrawaddy River, Burma, 100

Jadalpara Reserve, India, 104
Jaraguà Nature Reserve, Brazil, 117
Jonker's Hoek Nature Reserve, South Africa, 111

Kabalega Falls Nature Park, Uganda, 109, **109**, **113**
Kagera National Park, Ruanda, 109
Kampinos National Park, Poland, 99
Kasanga Reserve, Zambia, 111
Kaziranga National Park, India, 104
Kilombero Valley, Tanzania, 109
Kisbalaton Reserve, Hungary, 100
Kivu, Lake, Ruanda, 109
Kops Stansee Reserve, Austria, 99

Lanin National Park, Argentina, 117
Loch Druidibeg, Great Britain, 97
Loch Levan, Great Britain, 97

Lukanga Valley, Zambia, 111
Lunga Reserve, Zambia, 111

Macquarie Marsh, Australia, 105
Magadi, Lake, Kenya, 109
Magdalena River, Colombia, 114
Maidombe, Lake, Zaire, 107
Managua, Lake, Nicaragua, 114
Mana Pools Game Reserve, Rhodesia, 111
Manda Wildlife Park, Chad, 107
Maracaibo Lagoon, Venezuela, 114
Marchegg Nature Reserve, Austria, 99
Maritza Delta, Greece, 100
Merritt Island, Florida, USA, 112
Meru Reserve, Kenya, 109
Mississippi Delta, Louisiana, USA, 113
Missolonghi Lagoon, Greece, 100
Mnyara Lake National Park, Tanzania, 109
Mobutu Sese Seko, Lake, Uganda, 109
Morecambe Bay, Great Britain, 95, 97
Muddus National Park, Sweden, 99
Mweru, Lake, Zambia, 111
Mushandike National Park, Rhodesia, 111

Nakuru, Lake, Kenya, 109, **111**
Natron, Lake, Tanzania, 109
Naivasha, Lake, Kenya, 109, **111**
Nariva Marsh, Trinidad, 114
Neretva Delta, Yugoslavia, 100
Neuchâtel, Lake, Switzerland, 98
Neusidler, Austria, 99
Ngorongoro Reserve, Tanzania, 109, **111**
Niger Delta, Nigeria, 107
Niger River, Mali, 105
Nile River, Sudan, 105
Nile River, Uganda, **112**
Niokolo Koba National Park, Senegal, 105
Noda Sagiyama Park, Japan, 104

Okefenokee Swamp, Georgia, USA, 113
Orinoco Delta, Venezuela, 114
Ouse Washes, Great Britain, 97

Padjelanta National Park, Sweden, 99
Pantanal, Brazil, 117
Paraguay River, Paraguay, 117
Paris Wildlife Refuge, Tennessee, USA, 113
Pelican Island, USA, 113
Pendjari National Park, Benin, 107
Petèn, Guatemala, 114
Pilcomayo River, Paraguay, 117
Plitvicka Jezera National Park, Yugoslavia, 100
Po Valley, Italy, 75, 95

Prespa, Lake, Yugoslavia, 100
Provaglio d'Iseo, Italy, 94

Queen Elizabeth Park, Uganda, 109

Ravenna, Italy, **15**, 95
Razelm Lagoon, Rumania, 100
Rhine-Ouadi Achim Reserve, Chad, 107
Ribble, River, Great Britain, 95
Ringkøbing Fjord, Denmark, 99
Rio Dulce National Park, Guatemala, 114
Ropotamo Park, Bulgaria, 100
Ruaha National Park, Tanzania, 109
Rukwa Lake, Tanzania, 109

Saint Lucia Forest, South Africa, 111
Sambu Reserve, Zambia, 111
San Jorge River, Colombia, 114
San Lorenzo Park, Ecuador, 117
Savannah Refuge, South Carolina, USA, 113
Schleswig-Holstein, Lake, West Germany, 99
Scutari, Lake, Yugoslavia, 100
Shiretoko Park, Japan, 105
Siberia, Soviet Union, 100, **107**
Solway Firth, Great Britain, 97
Srebarna Park, Bulgaria, 100
Sukla Phanta, India, 104

Tanganyika, Lake, Tanzania, 109
Taroba Park, India, 104
Thau, River, France, 43
Titicaca, Lake, Peru, 117
Toro Game Reserve, Uganda, 109
Tsavo National Park, Kenya, 109
Tumba, Lake, Zaire, 109
Tuscany, Italy, 30, 75, 95

Umfolozi, South Africa, 111
Upemba National Park, Zaire, 109

Velence, Lake, Hungary, 100
Venice Lagoon, Italy, 15, **21**, 94
Victoria, Lake, Kenya, Tanzania, Uganda, 109
Victoca National Park, Bulgaria, 100
Volga Delta, Soviet Union, 100

Wash, The, Great Britain, 95
Waza National Park, Cameroun, 107
Wia-Wia Reserve, Guyana, 114

Yangtze Kiang, River, China, 105
Yankari Reserve, Nigeria, 107

Zakouma Wildlife Park, Chad, 107

Species Index

Page numbers for picture references are in bold type, Latin names in italics.

Acrocephalus scirpaceus, 88
A. palustris, 88
A. schoenobaenus, 88
A. paludicola, 88
A. arundinaceus, 88
Aix galericulata, 105
Alcedo atthis, 88
Aldrovando, 28
Alisma plantago-aquatica, 31
Alligator, Mississippi, **113**
Ammophila, 18
Amoebae, 43
Anas acuta, 87
A. crecca, 87

A. penelope, 87
A. platyrhynca, 67
A. querquedula, 87
A. strepera, 87
Anchovy, 42
Anopheles maculipennis, 9
Anser albifrons, 85
A. anser, 85
A. fabalis, 85
Ant, **54**
Aphid, **55**, 56
Aquila clanga, 89
A. pomarina, 90
Arca diluvii, 43

Ardea cinerea, 63, 68
A. purpurea, 63, 68
Ardeola ralloides, 72
Argentina, 117
Chaco, 117
Corrientes, 117
Lanin National Park, 117
Arrowhead, 31
Arvicola terrestris, 90
Asio flammeus, 90
A. otus, 90
Atherine, 42
Atherina mochon, 42
Australia, 105

Lake Albert, 105
Lake Alexandrina, 105
Lake Coorong, 105
Lake Hattah, 105
Austria, 99
Neusiedler, 99
Furtner Teich Nature Reserve, 99
Kops Stansee Nature Reserve, 99
Marchegg Nature Reserve, 99
Avocet, **76**, 78
Aythya ferina, 87
A. fuligula, 87
A. marila, 87
A. nyroca, 87

Azolla caroliniana, 31

Bittern, 73
  Little, **68**, 72
Boar, Wild, **90**, 90
Bog moss, 26
Bombina bombina, 59
  B. variegata, 59
Botaurus stellarus, 73
Bothus, 42
Brazil, 117
  Amazon, 32, 114, **117**
  Aparados de Serra National Park, 117
  Jaragua Nature Reserve, 117
  Pantanal, 117
Brill, 42
Brontosaurus, 39
Bubulcus ibis, 75
Bucephala clangula, 87
Bufo bufo, 59
Bulgaria, 100
  Srebana Park, 100
  Ropotamo Park, 100
  Victoca National Park, 100
Burma, 100
  Lake Inle, 100
Butomus umbellatus, 31
Butterfly, Camberwell Beauty, 55
  Swallowtail, **52**, 55

Caddisfly, 50
Cambodia, 100
  Angkor National Park, 100, **105**
Cameroun, 107
  Waza National Park, 107
Carcinus maenas, 43
Carex, 27
Carp, 57
Casmerodius albus, 72
Cat's tail, **32**, 32
Cavalluccio marino, 42
Ceresa bubalus, **56**
Cettia cetti, 88
Chad, 107
  Rhine–Ouadi Achim Reserve, 107
  Lake Chad, 107
Charadrius alexandrinus, 77
  C. dubius, 77
  C. hiaticula, 77
China, 105
  Yangtze Kiang River, 105
Chlidonias hybrida, 85
  C. niger, 85
Chlorella, 39
Chrysopa, 56
Ciconia ciconia, 75
Circus aeruginosus, 89
  C. pygargus, 89
Coccinella, 56
Coleoptera, 52, 57
Colombia, 114
  Cauca River, 114
  César River, 114
  Magdalena River, 114
  San Jorge River, 114
Coot, 67, **78**, **79**, 83
Cormorant, Black-feathered, 75
Crab, 43
Crangon, 43
Crocodile, **107**
  Nile, **113**
  Salt-water, 105
Crocodylus porosus, 105
Curlew, 76
Cyclops, 43
Cygnus atratus, 105
  C. cygnus, 85
  C. olor, 85
Cyperus papyrus, 32
Czechoslovakia, 100

Biskupice Reserve, 100
  Mrtvy Luh Reserve, 100

Dabchick, 83
Dama dama, 90
Daphnia cladoceri, 43
Deer, Fallow, 90
  Marsh, **104**
Denmark, 99
  Ringkøbing Fjord, 99
Dentex dentex, 42
Dionaea muscipula, 28
Diptera, 51
Dragonfly, 40, **45**, 52
  larva, **43**
Drosera, 28, **30**
Duck, Carolina Wood, **114**
  Ferruginous, 87
  Mandarin 105
  Tufted, 87
  White-headed, 87
  numbers in N. America, 68
Dytiscus marginalis, 45

Eagle, Fish, **89**
  Lesser Spotted, 90
  Spotted, 89
Ecuador, 117
  Guayaquil Gulf, 117
  Guayas River, 117
  San Lorenzo Park, 117
Eel, 57
Egret, 63, **67**
  Cattle, 75
Egretta garzetta, 63, 72
Elodea canadensis, 27
Emys orbicularis, 60
Engraulis encrasicholus, 42
Ephemeroptera, 51
Equisetum palustre, 31
Erotettix cyanae, 57
Esox lucius, 57
Ethiopia, 105
  Ethiopian Plateau, 105

Finland, 100
Flamingo, **72**, 75, **97**, 98, **111**
France, 97
  Camargue, **11**, **97**, 98, **99**
  Thau, 43
Frog, **41**, 41
  Edible, 57
  Green, **58**
  Tree, **59**, 59
Frog-bit, 29
Fulica atra, 67, 83

Gadwall, 87
Gallinago media, 76
  G. gallinago, 76
Gallinula chloropus, 85
Gallinule, Purple, 85
Gambusia, **50**
Gambusia affinis, 47
Garganey, 87
Ghana, 100
Glariola pratincola, 77
Gobius, 42
Goby, 42
Godwit, Bar-tailed, 76
  Black-tailed, 76
Goldeneye, 87
Goosander, 87
Goose, Bean, 85
  Greylag, 85
  White-fronted, 85
Grass, Cotton, **24**
  Knot, 27
  Marsh, 15, 18
  Tape, 27

Great Britain, 95
  River Dee, 97
  Morecambe Bay, 95
  Ouse Washes, 97
  River Ribble, 95
  Solway Firth, 97
  The Wash, 95
Grebe, **76**
  Giant, 114
  Great Crested, 82
Greece, 100
  Maritza Delta, 100
Guatemala, 114
  Lake Atitlàn, 114
  Peten, 114
  Rio Dulce, 114
Gull, Black-headed, 85
  Herring, 85, **87**
  Lesser Black-headed, 85
Gunnard, 42
Guyana, 114
  Wia-Wia Reserve, 114
Gyrinidae, 52

Haematopus ostralegus, 77
Haemopsis sanguisuga, 43
Halophytes, 21, 22
Harrier, Marsh, 89
  Montagu's, 89
Hemiptera, 57
Heodes disparcontinentalis, **52**, 55
Heron, 41, **50**, 62, 68, 94
  Blue-grey, 62, **67**, 68
  Goliath, **111**
  Green, **70**
  Little Blue, **70**
  Louisiana, **70**
  Night, 62, 75
  Purple, **65**, **67**, 68
  Squacco, **68**, 68, 72
  White, **70**, 72
Himantopus himantopus, 67, 77
Hippopotamus, **29**
Hirudo medicinalis, 43
Homoptera, 57
Horsefly, **51**, 51
Horsetail, 31
Hottonia palustris, 31
Hoverfly, **52**, 56
Hungary, 100
  Feher Reserve, 100
  Kisbalaton Reserve, 100
  Lake Velence, 100
Hydrocharis morsus-ranae, 29
Hyla arborea, 59

Ibis, Glossy, 75
  Scarlet, **114**
India, 104
  Bharatpur Reserve, 104
  Chitawan Park, 104
  Jadalpara Reserve, 104
  Kazirange National Park, 104
  Sukla Phanta, 104
  Taroba Park, 104
Indo-China, 100
Iris, Flag, **21**
Iris pseudacorus, 31
Italy, 94
  Belbo River, 94
  Bolgheri, **94**, 95
  Lake Candia, 94
  Comacchio Valley, **15**, 57, **95**
  Lake Como, 94
  Crescentino, 94
  Po Valley, 95
  Provaglio d'Iseo, 94
  Ravenna, **15**
  Tuscany, 95
  Venice Lagoon, 15, **21**, 94

Ivory Coast, 105
  Bouna Reserve, 105
Ixobrychus minutus, 72

Jacana, **114**
Japan, 104
  Hokkaido, 104
  Noda Sagiyama Park, 104
Juncus conglomeratus, 32
  J. maritimus, 22
Juniper, 18
Juniperus communis, 18
  J. macrocarpa, 18

Kenya, 109
  Aberdare National Park, 109
  Baringo Lake, **32**, 109
  Elmenteita Lake, 109
  Magadi Lake, 109
  Meru Reserve, 109
  Naivasha Lake, 109
  Nakuru Lake, 109, **111**
  Tsavo National Park, 109
  Lake Victoria, 109
Kingfisher, 88
  Black and White, **111**

Lacewing, 56
Ladybird, **54**, 56
Lamellibrancha (*Anodonta*), 45
  L. (*Unio*), 45
Lapwing, 77
Larus argentatus, 85
  L. fuscus, 85
  L. ridibundus, 85
Leech, 45
Lemna, 30
  L. minor, 30
  L. polyrrhiza, 31
Limnea, 45
  L. palustris, 41
  L. stagnalis, 45
Limosa lapponica, 76
  L. limosa, 76
Lobster, 43
Locustella lanceolata, 88
Lotus Flower, **26**
Lutra lutra, 90

Mackerel, 42
Malaria, 8
Mali, 105
  Lake Debo, 105
  River Niger, 105
Mallard, 67, **87**, 87
Mangrove, **22**, 22, 23
Mantis religiosa, 57
Marsilea quadrifolia, 31
Mayfly, 51
Merganser, Red-breasted, 87
Mergus merganser, 87
  M. serrator, 87
Micromys minutus, 90
Moorhen, **82**, 85
Mosquito, 8, 8, 9, 10, 47
  Spotted-wing, 9
  lavae and pupae, **38**
Mouse, Harvest, 90
Mozambique, 111
  Gorongoza National Park, 111
Mudfish, **57**
Mullet, 42
Mullus barbatus, 42
  M. surmuletus, 42
Murex trunculus, 43
Myosotis palustris, 31
Myriophyllum verticillatum, 28

Natrix maura, 60
  N. natrix, 60

Nelumbo luteum, 30
 N. nucifera, 29
Nepa rubra, 50
Netherlands, The, 98
 Texel, 98
 Netta rufina, 87
Newt, **60**
 Alpine, **60**
 Common, 60
New Zealand, 105
 Abel Tasman National Park, 105
 Egmont National Park, 105
Nicaragua, 114
 Lake Nicaragua, 114
Nigeria, 107
 Benin National Park, 107
 Lake Chad, 107
 Niger Delta, 107
 Yankari Reserve, 107
Norway, 99
 Fokstumyra Nature Reserve, 99
Notonecta glauca, 47
Numenius arquata, 76
Nuphar luteum, 29
Nycticorax nycticorax, 63, 75
Nymphea alba, 29
Nymphalid, 55
Nymphalis atalanta, 55
 N. antiopa, 55
 N. io, 55

Oblada melanura, 42
Odonata, 52
Omphalia, **24**
Oryctolagus cuniculus, 90
Osprey, 89
Otter, **90**, 90
Owl, Long-eared, **89**, 90
 Short-eared, 90
Oxyura leucocephala, 87
Oystercatcher, 77, **97**

Panurus biarmicus, 89
Papilio machaon, 55
Papyrus, **29**, 32
Paraguay, 117
 Chaco Boreal, 117
 Paraguay River, 117
 Pilcomayo River, 117
Paramecium, 43
Pelecanus crispus, 75
 P. onocrotalus, 75
Pelican, 75, **100**, **111**
 Dalmatian, 75
Pendion haliaetus, 89
Perla maxima, 51
Peru, 117
 Lake Titicaca, 117
Phalacrocorax carbo, 75
Philomachus pugnax, 75
Phoenicepterus ruber, 75
Phragmites, 22
 P. communis, 32
Pike, 57
Pine, 18
Pintail, 87
Pinus halepensis, 18
 P. pinea, 18
Pipefish, 42
Plankton, 20
 Phytoplankton, 39
 Zooplankton, 39
Planorbis, 45
Plasmodium, 9
Platalea leucorodia, 75
Plegadis falcinellus, 75
Plover, Kentish, 77
 Little Ringed, 77
 Ringed, 77
 Pochard, 87

Red-crested, 87
Podiceps cristatus, 82
 P. ruficolis, 83
Podilymbus gigas, 114
Poland, 99
 Bielowieza Forest National Park, 99
 Kampinos National Park, 99
Polygonum, 29
Porphyrio porphyrio, 85
Potamogeton, 29
Pratincole, 77
Praying Mantis, 57

Rabbit, 90
Rallus aquaticus, 85
Ramsar Conference, Iran, 11
Rana esculenta, 57
Ranatra linearis, 50
Recurvirostra avosetta, 78
Reed, Common, **20**
 Marsh, 32
Remiz pendulinus, 89
Rhinoceros, **100**
Rhizophora, 23
Rhodesia, 111
 Chimanimani National Park, 111
 Mana Pools National Park, 111
 Mushandike National Park, 111
Ruanda, 109
 Kager National Park, 109
 Kivu Lake, 109
Ruff, **72**, 75
Rumania, 100
 Danube Delta, 100
 Razelm Lagoon, 100
Rush, Flowering, **31**
 Marsh, 32

Sagittaria, 26
 S. sagittifolia, 31
Salcornia fruticosa, 20
 S. herbacea, 20
Salpa, 42
Salvinia, **27**, 117
 S. natans, 31
 S. rotundifolia, 31
Samphire, 20, **21**, 21, **90**
Sardine, 42
Sardinia, 98
Sardina pilchardus, 42
Scaup, 87
Scirpus lacuster, 32
 S. maritimus, 32
Scomber scomber, 42
Sea Bream, 42
Sea-horse, 42
Sea marshes, 15, 18
Seal, 95
Sedges, 27
Senegal, 105
 Djoval Nature Reserve, 105
 Niokolo Koba National Park, 105
Shank, Green, 76
 Red, 76
 Spotted Red, 76
Shoveler, 87
Shrimp, 41
Snail, Marsh, 41
 Pond, 39, 45
Snake, Grass, 63
Snipe, **73**, 76
 Great, 76
Sole, 42
Solea, 42
Solen vagina, 43
South Africa, 111
 Barberspan Reserve, 111
 Jonker's Hoek Nature Reserve, 111
 Saint Lucia Forest, 111
Soviet Union, 100

Astrakan Reserve, 100
 Siberia, 100, **107**
 Volga Delta, 100
Spatula clypeata, 87
Sphagnum, 26
Spain, 98
 Coto Donana Reserve, **13**, **98**, 98
 Guadalquivir River, **18**, 98, **99**
Spartina, 22
Spoonbill, 75
Starling, **87**, 88
Sterna albifrons, 85
 S. hirundo, 85
Stilt, Black-winged, 67, **73**, **75**, 77
Stonefly, 51
Stork, 75
 Indian Wood, **100**
Sturnus vulgaris, 88
Sudan, 105
 Nile River, 105
Sundew, 28
Sus scrofa, 90
Swan, Black, 105, **107**
 Mute, 85
 Whooper, 85
Sweden, 99
 Muddus National Park, 99
 Padjelanta National Park, 99
Switzerland, 98
 Alps, **32**
 Lake Geneva, 98
 Lake Neuchâtel, 98
Sympetrum sanguineum, **42**
Syngnathus acus, 42

Tadpoles, 59
Tanzania, 109
 Eyasi, Lake, 109
 Kilombero Valley, 109
 Ngorongoro Reserve, **111**
 Lake Natron, 109
 Ruaha National Park, 109
 Lake Rukwa, 109
 Lake Tanganyika, 109
 Lake Victoria, 109
Teal, 87
Tench, 57
Tern, **82**
 Common, 85
 Black, 85
 Little, 85
 Whiskered, 85
Tiger, Bengal, **104**
Tinca tinca, 57
Tit, Bearded, **88**, 89
 Penduline, **88**, 90
Tortoise, 61
 European Pond, 60
 Pond, **61**
Toad, Common, 59
 Fire-bellied, **58**, 59
 Tree, 59
Trapa natans, 30
Treehopper, 57
Trichoptera, 50
Triglia, 42
Tringa erythropus, 76
 T. flavipes, 76
 T. melanoleuca, 76
 T. nebularia, 76
 T. totanus, 76
Trinidad, Nariva Marsh, 114
Triturus alpestris, 60
 T. cristatus, 60
 T. vulgaris, 60
Tubifex tubifex, 43
Typha angustifolia, 32
 T. latifolia, 32

Uganda, 109

Lake Idi Amin Dada, 109
 Kabalega Falls, 109, **113**
 Lake Mobuto Sese Seko, 109
 Nile River, **112**
 Queen Elizabeth Park, 109
 Toro Game Reserve, 109
 Lake Victoria, 109
United States, 113
 Corkscrew Swamp Sanctuary, Florida, 113
 Everglades, Florida, 11, **32**, **90**, 111, **117**
 Lacassine Wildlife Refuge, Louisiana, 113
 Mississippi Delta, Louisiana, 113
 Merritt Island, Florida, 111
 Okefenokee Swamp, Georgia, 113
 Pelican Island, 113
 Savannah Wildlife Refuge, South Carolina, 113
Utricularia, 28

Vallisneria, 27
Vanellus vanellus, 77
Venezuela, 114
 Maracaibo Lagoon, 114
 Orinoco Delta, 114
Venus fly-trap, **31**
Venus verrucosa, 43
Victoria regia, **15**, 29, 117

Warbler, Aquatic, 88
 Cetti's, 88
 Great Reed, 88
 Marsh, 88
 Reed, 88
 Sedge, 88
 Temminck's Grasshopper, 88
Waders, 75
Water-Boatman, 47, **57**
Water Chestnut, 30
Water-ferns, 31
Water Forget-Me-Not, 31
Water-Flea, 43
Water-Lily, 26
 Yellow, **24**
 White, **24**
Water-Milfoil, 28
Water-Plantain, 31
Water-Rail, 85
Water-Scorpion, 50
Water Snake, **63**
Water-Strider, **47**, 54
Water-Violet, 31
Water Vole, 90
Weed, Canadian Water, 27
 Duck, 30
West Germany, 99
 Lake Constance, 99
 Lake Dümmer, 99
 Federsee, 99
 Lake Gelting Birk, 99
 Lake Schleswig-Holstein, 99
Wigeon, 87, 95, 97, 113

Yellowlegs, Greater, 76
 Lesser, 76
Yugoslavia, 100
 Neretva Delta, 100
 Plitvicka Jezera National Park, 100
 Lake Prespa, 100
 Lake Scutari, 100

Zaire, 109
 Albert National Park, 109
 Lake Tumba, 109
 Upemba National Park, 109
Zambia, 111
 Lake Bangweulu, 111
 Kasanga Reserve, 111
 Lukanga Valley Reserve, 111
 Lunga Reserve, 111
 Mweru Lake Reserve, 111